UNITED STATES
ARMY WAR COLLEGE
PRESS

Carlisle Barracks, PA STRENGTH—WISDOM

THE RISE OF IWAR:
IDENTITY, INFORMATION, AND THE
INDIVIDUALIZATION OF MODERN WARFARE

Glenn J. Voelz

U.S. ARMY WAR COLLEGE

SSI
STRATEGIC STUDIES INSTITUTE

First published 2015 by the Strategic Studies Institute and US Army War College Press.
First Skyhorse edition 2018.

Skyhorse Publishing books may be purchased in bulk at special discounts for sales promotion, corporate gifts, fund-raising, or educational purposes. Special editions can also be created to specifications. For details, contact the Special Sales Department, Skyhorse Publishing, 307 West 36th Street, 11th Floor, New York, NY 10018 or info@skyhorsepublishing.com.

Visit our website at www.skyhorsepublishing.com.

10 9 8 7 6 5 4 3 2 1

Library of Congress Cataloging-in-Publication Data is available on file.

Cover design by Rain Saukas
Cover photo credit iStock

ISBN: 978-1-5107-2605-5
Ebook ISBN: 978-1-5107-2617-8

Printed in the United States of America

The United States Army War College

The United States Army War College educates and develops leaders for service at the strategic level while advancing knowledge in the global application of Landpower.

The purpose of the United States Army War College is to produce graduates who are skilled critical thinkers and complex problem solvers. Concurrently, it is our duty to the U.S. Army to also act as a "think factory" for commanders and civilian leaders at the strategic level worldwide and routinely engage in discourse and debate concerning the role of ground forces in achieving national security objectives.

The Strategic Studies Institute publishes national security and strategic research and analysis to influence policy debate and bridge the gap between military and academia.

The Center for Strategic Leadership and Development contributes to the education of world class senior leaders, develops expert knowledge, and provides solutions to strategic Army issues affecting the national security community.

The Peacekeeping and Stability Operations Institute provides subject matter expertise, technical review, and writing expertise to agencies that develop stability operations concepts and doctrines.

The Senior Leader Development and Resiliency program supports the United States Army War College's lines of effort to educate strategic leaders and provide well-being education and support by developing self-awareness through leader feedback and leader resiliency.

The School of Strategic Landpower develops strategic leaders by providing a strong foundation of wisdom grounded in mastery of the profession of arms, and by serving as a crucible for educating future leaders in the analysis, evaluation, and refinement of professional expertise in war, strategy, operations, national security, resource management, and responsible command.

The U.S. Army Heritage and Education Center acquires, conserves, and exhibits historical materials for use to support the U.S. Army, educate an international audience, and honor Soldiers—past and present.

STRATEGIC STUDIES INSTITUTE

The Strategic Studies Institute (SSI) is part of the U.S. Army War College and is the strategic-level study agent for issues related to national security and military strategy with emphasis on geostrategic analysis.

The mission of SSI is to use independent analysis to conduct strategic studies that develop policy recommendations on:

- Strategy, planning, and policy for joint and combined employment of military forces;

- Regional strategic appraisals;

- The nature of land warfare;

- Matters affecting the Army's future;

- The concepts, philosophy, and theory of strategy; and,

- Other issues of importance to the leadership of the Army.

Studies produced by civilian and military analysts concern topics having strategic implications for the Army, the Department of Defense, and the larger national security community.

In addition to its studies, SSI publishes special reports on topics of special or immediate interest. These include edited proceedings of conferences and topically oriented roundtables, expanded trip reports, and quick-reaction responses to senior Army leaders.

The Institute provides a valuable analytical capability within the Army to address strategic and other issues in support of Army participation in national security policy formulation.

Strategic Studies Institute
and
U.S. Army War College Press

THE RISE OF IWAR:
IDENTITY, INFORMATION,
AND THE INDIVIDUALIZATION
OF MODERN WARFARE

Glenn J. Voelz

October 2015

*****

Comments pertaining to this report are invited and should be forwarded to: Director, Strategic Studies Institute and U.S. Army War College Press, U.S. Army War College, 47 Ashburn Drive, Carlisle, PA 17013-5010.

*****

*****

*****

All sources and materials used in the research of this monograph were drawn from unclassified government documents, media reports, and open source literature.

*****

The author would like to thank a number of individuals and organizations providing important assistance and feedback during the course of this research. Foremost are the faculty, students, and staff of the Security Studies Program at the Massachusetts Institute of Technology (MIT) and MIT's Lincoln Laboratory for their support and generosity during the author's fellowship.

A number of organizations hosted the author for general discussions on identity, technology, and broader issues relating to national security strategy. These include the Defense Forensics and Biometrics Agency, the Defense Forensic Science Center, U.S. Special Operations Command, the Army Deputy Chief of Staff for Intelligence, the National Ground Intelligence Center, the National Media Exploitation Center, the Identity Intelligence Project of the Office of the Defense Intelligence Agency, and several offices within the Director of National Intelligence. The author also benefitted greatly from dozens of professional discussions and seminars presented during the 2014 Global Identity Summit.

In particular, the author would like to acknowledge the significant support of Ed Wack at MIT's Lincoln Laboratory, Jim Shufelt of the U.S. Army War College, and Dr. Barry Posen and Dr. Owen Cote of MIT's Security Studies Program. Their support and critique of the ideas developed in this monograph have been invaluable. Any errors of fact or analysis are the author's alone.

FOREWORD

During a recent address to the National Defense University on U.S. counterterrorism strategy, President Barack Obama cautioned that "we must define the nature and scope of this struggle, or else it will define us." His comments hinted at the dramatic transformations of the U.S. military and national security apparatus since September 11, 2001 (9/11). Notable among these have been a new operational emphasis on the threats posed by nonstate actors and individual combatants. This trend represents a major shift from the Cold War era paradigm focused primarily on conventional threats from state-based adversaries. This strategic reprioritization has evolved into new military doctrines focused on the task of defeating networks rather than formations and technical innovations designed for identifying, screening, and targeting individual combatants on the battlefield. This operational focus has also made the issue of identity central to U.S. national security strategy—whether screening individual threats at the borders, segregating them on the battlefield, or targeting them across the spaces in between.

In this monograph, Colonel Glenn Voelz examines this defining feature of recent conflicts, specifically the doctrinal and technical innovations giving rise to this new operational paradigm. He describes the central pillars of individualized warfare, including the rise of identity-based targeting and the key role of information technology in conducting these operations. This work contributes to an important dialogue concerning lessons learned from a decade of global counterterrorism operations and two extended counterinsurgency campaigns. It provides a useful case study on wartime military innovation by considering the policies and strategies that evolved in response to a new and unexpected adversary. He concludes this monograph with an in-depth discussion covering a range of emerging technologies likely to define how this kind of war will be waged in the future.

DOUGLAS C. LOVELACE, JR.
Director
Strategic Studies Institute and
    U.S. Army War College Press

ABOUT THE AUTHOR

GLENN J. VOELZ is an Army intelligence officer and most recently the U.S. Army War College fellow at the Massachusetts Institute of Technology (MIT) Security Studies Program and MIT's Lincoln Laboratory. He currently serves in the Intelligence Division of the International Military Staff at the North Atlantic Treaty Organization headquarters in Brussels, Belgium. During his career, Colonel Voelz has served in various positions at the Defense Intelligence Agency, on the Joint Chiefs of Staff at the Pentagon, and as the Senior Duty Officer in the White House Situation Room. His military duties have included assignments in Asia, Africa, the Middle East, and Europe. He previously served as an Assistant Professor of History at West Point. Early in his career, he was a member of the Army's World Class Athlete Program and was a two-time U.S. Olympic Trials qualifier for Swimming in 1988 and in Modern Pentathlon in 1996. Colonel Voelz is the author of several books and journal articles on a range of topics including diplomatic history, government contracting, intelligence policy, and military strategy. Colonel Voelz is a graduate of West Point where he was commissioned as an Infantry officer in 1992. He holds advanced degrees from the University of Virginia and the National Intelligence University in Washington, DC.

SUMMARY

During a decade of global counterterrorism operations and two extended counterinsurgency campaigns, the United States was confronted with a new kind of adversary. Without uniforms, flags, and formations, the task of identifying and targeting these combatants represented an unprecedented operational challenge for which Cold War era doctrinal methods were largely unsuited. This dilemma became the catalyst for a decade of doctrinal, technical, and organizational change premised on the central idea that nonstate actors and individual combatants were a salient national security concern and, therefore, legitimate military targets. This strategic reprioritization evolved into a new model of state warfare centered on the operational tasks of identifying, screening, and targeting individual combatants and defeating their networks.

This mode of warfare has been characterized by analytical methods focused on the systematic disaggregation of threats down to the lowest possible level — often the individual combatant on the battlefield. When irregular adversaries could no longer be differentiated by uniform or status, identity attributes became the new technical signature of battlefield targeting. Biographic, biometric, and forensics data became a critical component of the targeting process. The collection and analysis of this data required new information management technologies designed to reduce anonymity on the battlefield, penetrate complex networks, and differentiate friend from foe. This also required architectures able to process and communicate identity data across the entire national security apparatus.

This monograph examines the doctrinal, technical, and bureaucratic innovations that evolved in response to these new operational challenges. It examines the transition from a conventionally focused, Cold War-era targeting process to one optimized for combating networks and conducting identity-based targeting. It analyzes the policy decisions and strategic choices that were the catalysts of this change and concludes with an in-depth examination of emerging technologies that are likely to shape how this mode of warfare will be waged in the future.

THE RISE OF IWAR:
IDENTITY, INFORMATION, AND THE INDIVIDUALIZATION OF MODERN WARFARE

Whenever you want to attack an army, besiege a city, or kill a person, first you must know the identities of their defending generals, their associates, their visitors, their gatekeepers, and their chamberlains . . .

Sun Tzu, *The Art of War*[1]

INTRODUCTION

In late-2014, the United States reached the milestone of the 500th nonbattlefield targeted strike, operations that have killed some 3,600 people over the last decade.[2] Beyond the numbers, this event is notable as one example of a new mode of state warfare based on military power being applied directly against individual combatants rather than formations. These so-called "targeted killings" are perhaps the most vivid example of the individualization of American warfare. The commander in chief now routinely reviews and approves strikes against named combatants, a phenomenon "without precedent in presidential history."[3] However, this trend is not limited only to high-level counterterrorism efforts. It reflects a new strategic calculus that has elevated the status of the individual combatant into a foremost concern of national security policy and made the targeting of these entities a major driver of doctrinal and technical innovation on the battlefield.

The attacks of September 11, 2001 (9/11) and two extended counterinsurgency campaigns presented the United States with adversaries for which it was largely unprepared. These new opponents did not fight as conventional formations or within a clearly defined battle space. Rather, they were organized as distributed networks and small cells, composed of individuals often indistinguishable from the surrounding population. Without uniforms and flags, the task of identifying and targeting these entities presented an unprecedented operational challenge for which traditional warfighting approaches were largely unsuited. In response, the U.S. national security apparatus embarked upon a decade of doctrinal, technical, and organizational innovation premised on the central idea that individual combatants represented a salient national security concern and legitimate military target. Within this new operational paradigm, the identification, screening, and targeting of "high-value individuals" and their associated networks became the focus of a new mode of state warfare—iWar.

THE PILLARS OF IWAR

The rise of iWar is a case study of military innovation centered on the operational task of identifying, screening, and targeting individual combatants and their networks; iWar is characterized by three distinct elements: **Individualization**, **Identity**, and **Information**. These pillars provide a conceptual framework for analyzing the dramatic changes in doctrine, technology, and strategic focus that have redefined how the United States wages war abroad and protects its borders at home.

- **Individualization**: Over the last decade, the U.S. national security apparatus shifted from its traditional focus on conventional military adversaries to an emphasis on nonstate threats and opponents fighting as dispersed, highly adaptive networks. This reorientation led to the adoption of new analytical methods and operational approaches based on the systematic disaggregation of threats down to the lowest possible level—often the individual combatant. In this mode of warfare, the targeting of "high-value individuals" became a paramount national security concern and key driver of doctrinal and technical innovation on the battlefield.

- **Identity**: As networked adversaries and individual combatants moved to the focal point of warfighting and domestic security concerns, there was a pressing need to identify and discriminate among these entities. In the age of iWar, the opponents were no longer generic soldiers who could be differentiated on the basis of status or uniform. As the targeting process became personalized, new kinds of information and methods were required which included biographic, biometric, and forensics data, and the use of network analysis for linking these identities to places, activities, and other actors. Identity attributes became the new technical signature of battlefield targeting and the first line of defense in the "watch listing" approach to homeland security.

- **Information**: Waging iWar depended upon a revolution of information management built around technologies designed for differentiating individual actors on the battlefield and segregating friend from foe. These tasks were unlike the analytical challenges of industrial age warfare and required new tools and methods for collecting, processing, and communicating identity information across the entire national security apparatus. The need to identify, screen, and target these threats at home and abroad made information management and data analysis the most important weapons in the age of iWar.

These pillars of iWar reflect a new operational paradigm that emerged in response to an unexpected adversary that fought as networks rather than formations. These combatants were not easily identifiable on the battlefield and used anonymity for operational advantage. Their activities were not limited to clearly defined battlefields or military targets. These characteristics enabled them to resist an overwhelming American advantage in conventional maneuver warfare, airpower, and logistics. This dilemma became the catalyst for a major reorientation of national security strategy based on the need to identify, screen, and target these individual combatants and their networks.

Within this new paradigm, operational progress could not be measured by the destruction of an adversary's physical infrastructure or control of key terrain. This paradox led the United States toward a strategy of tactics, one based on the systematic disaggregation of threats down to the lowest possible level. This approach evolved into warfighting methods that turned "the fusion of operations and intelligence for the purpose of hunting high-value targets into a high art."[4] In the waging of iWar, operational success has been defined by identifying these individual threats around the globe, segregating them on the battlefields, screening them at the borders, and targeting them across the spaces in between.

4

The tools and methods of iWar did not evolve as a result of grand overarching design. Rather, the pathway of innovation was defined by operational contingency, tactical adaptation, and new strategic priorities that emerged in response to an unexpected adversary. This led to a decade of significant doctrinal and technical innovation centered on the task of identifying and targeting threats from nonstate actors and individual combatants. This spurred an unprecedented revolution of information management and data sharing across the entire national security apparatus. It also fed major bureaucratic transformations that gradually eroded many of the traditional lines separating military operations, foreign intelligence activities, and domestic security functions. Together, these changes reflect a new strategic calculus that has placed threats from nonstate actors and individual combatants on equal footing with adversarial states as a driver of U.S. national security policy and military innovation.

RESEARCH FOCUS

This monograph is structured in two parts. The first section examines iWar as a case study of military innovation. It traces the course of doctrinal, technological, and organizational change within the U.S. national security apparatus in response to a new kind of adversary. It analyzes the dynamics of the post-9/11 security environment, identifying specific policy decisions and strategic choices that became the catalysts of change and drivers of innovation. It examines how these changes evolved from the very specific operational challenge of identifying, screening, and targeting individual combatants on the battlefield and at the borders. Finally, it demonstrates how these changes challenged many of the underlying presumptions that have guided the conduct of state warfare in the modern age.

The second part is more technically focused and speculative. It continues on the theme of military innovation by considering where current technical trends may lead as the United States continues to face threats from nonstate adversaries and individual actors. The monograph concludes with a scenario-based discussion that examines several emerging technology areas that may define how iWar is waged in the next generation.

THE CATALYSTS OF IWAR

The attacks of 9/11 largely debunked two enduring presumptions concerning the U.S. national security strategy of the post-Cold War era. The first was the traditional view that a combination of domestic social-cultural cohesion, stability among neighbors, and maritime separation could isolate the American homeland from the worst dangers emanating from failed states and transnational terrorism. A second presumption was that overwhelming strength in traditional war-fighting approaches based on maneuver warfare and firepower could deter the main threats to U.S. national security. However, the rise of al-Qaeda, two extended counterinsurgency campaigns, and persistent domestic security threats posed by nonstate actors served to challenge both of these presumptions.

In the aftermath of 9/11, the intelligence community, military, and homeland security entities faced a new kind of adversary that did not answer to a sovereign state, wear uniforms, or seek clearly defined geopolitical objectives. The nature of such threats had been articulated in various writings during the post-Cold War transition period, perhaps most prophetically in John Arquilla and David Ronfeldt's *Networks and Netwars*. In this work, the authors described nonstate actors organized as decentralized hybrid structures, engaging in low-intensity conflicts by leveraging doctrines and technologies based on network design.[5] Under the guise of "fourth generation warfare," William Lind, T. X. Hammes, and others foresaw these networks and individual actors potentially supplanting the state as drivers of a new global order, an idea later sensationalized by Thomas Friedman's thesis on "super empowered individuals."[6]

All of these writers highlighted the fact that combating such adversaries would require that states rethink doctrines and technologies that were ill-suited for operations in a nonlinear battle space dominated by networks and information campaigns rather than formations and conventional maneuver. They described an emerging security environment defined by conflicts between state and nonstate actors, or states using nonstate actors as proxies.[7] The common link among these predictions was the fact that these new adversaries would be structured as distributed networks rather than hierarchies. Conflicts would be sub-national or transnational in scope, and operations would tend to merge the strategic and tactical levels of war. Most importantly, these adversaries would be inherently difficult to identify and challenging to target. Defeating them would require new analytical approaches, organizational structures, technologies, and warfighting strategies.

Many of the *Netwar* predictions have since been validated by U.S. experience in Iraq and Afghanistan, the ongoing campaign against global terrorism, and, more recently, in so-called "hybrid conflicts" characterized by decentralized and irregular warfighting waged by militias rather than professional armies. In all of these endeavors, the United States has struggled to contain and defeat adversaries operating under an organizational logic far different from the highly formalized and doctrinally based threats of the Cold War era. Instead, these new adversaries have been structurally complex and notably lacking obvious operational centers of gravity. These entities employ highly idiosyncratic tactics and adaptive strategies that have been difficult to analyze, template, and counter. Additionally, they have been particularly adept at exploiting commercial technologies, communications, and financial networks to expand influence. In some cases, they approach "state-like disruptive capacity" in their ability to execute attacks with global impact.

The demands of waging this new kind of war presented a far different challenge than that of Cold War era adversaries. Prior to 9/11, U.S. intelligence methods still primarily reflected a legacy "order of battle" paradigm focused on units, equipment, formations, and fixed doctrinal templates. Collection priorities were focused on long-term technical analysis of threat capabilities and the monitoring of strategic indications and warnings. However, the U.S. campaigns in Iraq and Afghanistan demanded an entirely new approach with greater emphasis on "human terrain" and network analysis. The population centric approaches of counterinsurgency required "not only the ability to positively identify individuals within the population, but also to understand social structure in terms of the social relationships among the population."[8] As a result, the intelligence community and military forces underwent a major transformation based on warfighting theories that placed networks at the center of the analytical and operational challenge. This also meant that for the first time in modern American warfare, the issue of identity became a key data point and an operational "signature" that was critical for screening, segregating, and targeting individual combatants on the battlefield and stopping them at the borders.

iWar as National Security Strategy.

iWar was not born of specific design or as premeditated strategy. Instead, it evolved in piecemeal fashion as a result of ad hoc adaptations and incremental policy choices in the years following 9/11. The pillars of iWar have emerged at the center of the nation's counterterrorism targeting methods, in the warfighting approaches adopted in Iraq and Afghanistan, and as the basis of a homeland security strategy built on the foundation of identity-based screening.

The Authorization for Use of Military Force (AUMF) provided an important initial catalyst for iWar in authorizing use of force against "nations, organizations, or **persons**," thus setting the legal precedent for the targeting of individual combatants as an element of the nation's broader counterterrorism strategy. This policy choice eventually manifested into a strategy of focused counterterrorism raids, so-called "targeted killings," most notably by means of drone strikes in Pakistan, Yemen, and Somalia against top-tier leadership targets and key operational figures. This targeting methodology was gradually refined over time, particularly the shift from generic, signature-based targeting toward more highly focused "personality" strikes against specifically named individuals.

On the domestic front, the rise of iWar has been most evident in the emergence of the "watch listing" phenomena and identity-based screening programs that have become the central feature of post-9/11 homeland security strategy. Over the last decade, the identities of millions of individuals have been added to such watch lists, augmented with detailed biographic information, biometric profiles, operational histories, and extended networks of associations and contacts. These databases have become the informational basis of an identity-based screening program designed to spotlight individual threats and screen against likely risks to transportation networks, critical infrastructure, and domestic security.

Beyond counterterrorism targeting and homeland defense, the iWar paradigm has perhaps been most evident in the evolution of military doctrine, technologies, and warfighting approaches used in Iraq and Afghanistan. The population-centric approaches and targeting methods that gradually evolved during these campaigns were deeply influenced by network theory and analytical methods emphasizing the role of low-level groups, key influencers, and individual actors as critical variables in establishing local security. This operational focus led to a decade of rapid military technology innovation that introduced a range of new tools to the battlefield specifically designed to support identity management and personality-based targeting, including drones, biometrics, forensics, and advanced data processing systems. This new paradigm represented a major reorientation of military focus away from conventional warfighting methods toward a new model of state warfare centered on the identification, screening, and targeting of individual combatants.

iWar as a New Model of State Warfare.

Beyond new technologies and doctrines, the rise of iWar represents a profound departure from the foundational presumptions of the Westphalian system that has defined the context of state warfare for over 300 years since the end of the Thirty Years War. This historical moment marked an important transition point from the age of private mercenary conflicts toward a modern construct of warfare in which combatants came to be viewed as instruments of the state, acting on behalf of political sovereigns.[9] This symbolized a "depersonalization" of conflict as soldiers assumed collective identity as members of professional armies. Jean-Jacques Rousseau's seminal treatise on political power best articulated the significance of this transition, noting that modern warfare was no longer a:

> relationship between one man and another, but a relationship between one state and another, in which individuals are enemies only by accident, not as men, nor even as citizens, but as soldiers.[10]

This conceptualization provided the intellectual foundation for subsequent development of legal categorizations governing treatment of prisoners, wounded soldiers, civilians on the battlefield, and the basis for defining lawful combatency. Thus, under the Westphalian construct, soldiers became "generic" members of their national armies in terms of legal status and appearance. Uniforms emerged to distinguish soldiers from civilians and provide the operational context for lawful targeting and wartime protections.[11] Within this mode of warfare, combatant privileges, obligations, and rules of engagement were no longer linked to individual identity but rather to a soldiers' generic status as the member of a state formation.[12] Over time, this evolved into a normative framework governing the conduct of state warfare and conventions of military targeting.

Since 9/11, this construct has been directly challenged by a series of U.S. conflicts waged against networks rather than nations, with opposing forces comprised of "unprivileged enemy belligerents."[13] In this context the United States has conducted persistent battlefield operations against fighters who are legally disqualified from the privileges of combatant status as a result of joining or substantially supporting nonstate armed groups in the conduct of hostilities. This has created operational ambiguity where the traditional logic of status-based targeting no longer functions in practice. In its place, the U.S. military has evolved toward highly individualized approaches to threat assessment and identity-based targeting where adversaries are no longer "generic" fighters.

This new operational paradigm reflects a personalization of warfare where the legitimate use of military force has become "tied to quasi-adjudicative judgments about the individual acts and roles of specific enemy figures."[14] Targeting is increasingly based on an individuated assessment of specific combatants, determined through evidentiary analysis and weighing operational relevance within a larger network apparatus. This represents a dramatic transformation in the targeting criteria applied on the modern battlefield. This has also changed how information is gathered, analyzed, and used in support of military operations, such as the emergence of "evidence-based targeting."[15]

The rise of iWar has also challenged another tacit norm of the Westphalian construct, specifically the general prohibition against direct targeting of political leadership as a tactic of modern warfare. With the rise of professional militaries, political leaders no longer led armies directly into battle, thus creating a clear differentiation between those who conduct war at the policy level versus those who wage it on the battlefield.[16] The practical implication has been that "leadership strikes" against political figures or nonoperational targets generally have not evolved as a central component of military strategy.[17] However, this convention has been complicated by the ambiguity of distinguishing between operational and "political" leadership among nonstate groups. For instance, the United States has conducted lethal targeting against individuals variously described as religious leaders or spokesmen associated with extremist groups on the grounds that such individuals provide substantive support for terrorism activity. Yet, conventional interpretations of the law of armed conflict generally limit targeting to those directly participating in hostilities, while exempting individuals such as religious personnel or other civilians functioning in nonoperational roles. The iWar paradigm has complicated these distinctions, as status-based or functional criteria no longer offer a clear template for targeting these individual combatants.

There are also larger policy implications as individual combatants rather than conventional formations become the focus of operational targeting. The iWar paradigm has created an arbitrary zone of conflict with few discernable geopolitical, jurisdictional, or temporal boundaries, a fact tacitly acknowledged by successive U.S. administrations.[18] As one observer recently noted, a war against a constantly changing set of actors, moving freely from place to place and from organization to organization, can have no clearly defined "enemy" and does not end with a peace treaty.[19] Within such a conflict the categories of **battlefield**, **combatant**, and **hostilities** "no longer have clear or stable meaning."[20] This dilemma has been acutely demonstrated in the ongoing diplomatic and legal controversies surrounding nonbattlefield targeting and the issue of indefinite military detention.

Under the Westphalian construct, war termination occurs within a recognized framework, negotiated by terms of peace, and a normalized process for orderly demobilization and repatriation of combatants. However, campaigns in the age of iWar have not adhered to these traditional conventions. These conflicts have produced cohorts of wayfarer warriors, eager to apply their skills and experience across multiple theaters of conflict and acts of terrorism directed outside of recognized combat zones. This situation fundamentally has changed the operational significance of identity and necessitated strategies based on continuous monitoring of career fighters, both on and off the battlefield. Recidivism and a persistent global circulation of fighters have presented an entirely new security dilemma for nation-states, one that does not offer any clear path toward conventional military victory or orderly demobilization of combatants.

This situation reflects what some observers have called a hybridization of warfare as military operations increasingly span a broad spectrum of activities existing between the extremes of war and peace. As a mode of state conflict, iWar occupies this gray area between conventional warfare and law enforcement, sharing characteristics of both, yet without the procedural norms and clear legal context of either. For the United States, this has been characterized by the concurrent, and often integrated, use of traditional military measures such as kinetic strikes and battlefield detention, combined with law enforcement-like approaches based on evidentiary analysis, arrest, and prosecution. These methods evolved largely as a default solution for waging war across an unbounded battle space where "combatants" could be encountered on a battlefield as well as in an airport boarding queue. Indeed, some scholars have observed that this new mode of conflict, waged by state armies against individual combatants, has no existing legal framework upon which to base lawful targeting decisions.[21] Indeed, the operational trend toward highly personalized, identity-based targeting has challenged many of the conventions that have informed the use of military force by state powers for generations.

In sum, the rise of iWar represents a new mode of state warfare where the threat of individual combatants and networks supplanted conventional formations at the focal point of national security strategy. The next section examines iWar as an example of doctrinal innovation and considers how approaches to warfighting evolved since 9/11 in response to this new kind of adversary.

iWar as a Driver of Doctrinal Innovation.

The pillars of the iWar paradigm are clearly visible through the last decade of doctrinal innovation, particularly with regard to U.S. approaches to counterterrorism and counterinsurgency strategies. While these missions represent a distinct set of objectives and methods, on a conceptual level they share an important commonality in placing networks and individual actors at the center of the analytical and operational challenge. Examination of this doctrinal progression is a useful exercise for understanding how these concepts evolved over time into the military's institutional thinking. These doctrinal shifts provide important perspective into how organizational leaders understood the nature of post-9/11 adversaries and the methods needed to defeat them.

Among the early lessons of the campaigns in Iraq and Afghanistan was that "conventional warfare approaches often were ineffective when applied to operations other than major combat, forcing leaders to realign the ways and means of achieving effects."[22] The Army's recent targeting manual notes how the operational focus of conventional warfare "is to find and destroy ships, tank formations, or infrastructure." Conversely, the manual observes that, in counterinsurgency, the most difficult task is simply determining who is the enemy.[23] Reflecting these new operational challenges, a 2007 report by the Defense Science Board observed that the task of distinguishing combatant identities had become an increasingly important concern on the battlefield, particularly as status-based signatures "diminish in incidence and usefulness."[24]

These challenges led the U.S. military to undertake a decade of major doctrinal change focused on finding better methods for waging war against networks rather than formations, and targeting individual combatants rather than platforms. Even as U.S. forces embraced counterinsurgency theory with emphasis on governance and stability measures, much of the day-to-day operational focus in both Iraq and Afghanistan gravitated toward highly refined targeting efforts designed to "identify and separate the reconcilables from the irreconcilables."[25] A key component of establishing local security in these campaigns focused on aggressive efforts to identify and segregate key actors within insurgent networks, neutralize their networks, and conduct kill/capture operations against top-tier targets.

The "Find, Fix, Finish, Exploit, Analyze, and Disseminate" (F3EAD) targeting approach evolved as the preferred methodology for identifying and engaging these high-value individuals (HVI).[26] U.S. forces in both Iraq and Afghanistan applied the F3EAD process with great success against insurgent networks and terrorist cells. In Iraq, these network-based targeting approaches were used to develop all-source intelligence and provide "situational awareness of the local environment, its social networks, key decision-makers, and their motivations." This approach was perhaps most famously applied during the effort to track, target, and kill terrorist leader Abu Musab al-Zarqawi.[27] In support of future operations, General Stanley McChrystal described a tightly integrated operational process based on:

> analysts who found the enemy, drone operators who fixed the target; combat teams who finished the target by capturing or killing him; specialists who exploited the intelligence the raid yielded, such as cell phones, maps, and detainees; and the intelligence analysts who turned this raw information into usable knowledge.[28]

In Afghanistan, between 2009 and 2011, similar approaches were applied in targeting insurgent networks, using methods that enabled a five-fold increase in focused raids designed to capture or kill individual, high-level insurgents.[29] Beyond active combatants, these methods were also applied for nonkinetic targeting against drug producers and criminal networks as a means of undermining financial support to insurgent networks. Since then F3EAD has migrated into the military's conventional targeting doctrine and become part of the military's institutional training programs.[30]

While the F3EAD model was developed specifically as a process approach for personality-based targeting, it evolved within a larger conceptual framework based on Attack the Network (AtN) theory. AtN is a prime example of doctrinal evolution centered on micro-level disaggregation of the battlefield and network-based analysis in support of targeting. AtN emerged originally as an analytical approach for combating improvised explosive device (IED) networks and was designed for focused offensive operations against complex networks comprised of financiers, IED makers, trainers, and supporting infrastructure. AtN emphasized the use of specialized intelligence resources and analytical methods for identifying critical nodes and associational links within an adversary's network.[31] As part of this process, AtN offered a framework sub-categorizing individual actors within a tiered schema of target prioritization. For example, tier-one targets included top-level leadership, tier-two targets were intermediaries with links to facilitators and the population, and tier-three targets were primarily low-skilled foot soldiers and general threats among the population. Variations of this basic approach have been applied against a broad range of missions, such as tracking Joseph Koni and Lord's Resistance Army elements in Uganda, analyzing the spread of Boko Haram influence in Nigeria, and understanding threat finance patterns of narcotics traffickers in Latin America.

The development of F3EAD and AtN methods reflected the larger theoretical evolution and integration of Social Network Analysis (SNA) into the military's doctrinal cannon. The use of SNA for deconstructing the structure of complex networks predates the recent use by the U.S. military with scholarly research dating back to the 1960s. Notable among these early pioneers was Stanley Milgram's work on the "small-world" phenomenon and theories of structural disintermediation describing the dynamics of complex social networks.[32] More recently, researchers such as Duncan Watts broadened the application of network theory by demonstrating its relevance to phenomena such as disease contagion, consumer behavior, and the dynamics of social influence.[33] During the 1990s, SNA methods came into wider use for law enforcement and crime pattern analysis; however, they remained somewhat on the margins of military doctrinal thinking.[34] Admiral Arthur Cebrowski was among the first military leaders to apply these concepts directly to warfighting strategy in his influential work, *Network Centric Warfare*. He proposed a network-based concept of warfare using distributed sensors and precision targeting; however, at the time, he did not conceive of such methods being used specifically in the context of counterinsurgency or targeting of individual combatants.

The attacks of 9/11 became a primary catalyst for bringing SNA methods fully into the mainstream professional discourse on military strategy and targeting. Early works, such as Marc Sageman's *Understanding Terror Networks*, explicitly applied SNA as a framework for understanding a new kind of adversary. The 2006 publication of the influential Army counterinsurgency manual reflected these influences and brought SNA methods fully into the doctrinal cannon.[35] John Nagl one of the architects of this doctrine, observed that the inclusion of SNA methods played a critical role in driving:

> the Army's intelligence system away from a focus on analysis of conventional enemy units toward a personality-based understanding of the networks of super-empowered individuals . . .[36]

The new counterinsurgency manual described SNA as "a powerful threat evaluation tool" and introduced a new vocabulary into the military's operational vernacular, including concepts such as core-periphery structure, density, centrality, cohesion, clustering, and network visualization. These ideas were directly applied to the task of analyzing terrorist and insurgent networks, and identifying key actors and influencers on the battlefield.[37] The salient idea of applying SNA to the targeting process was how the "capture of one highly connected insurgent" from within a dense insurgent network could help counterinsurgents systematically neutralize the larger organizational structure.[38]

Within the context of counterinsurgency and counterterrorism operations, SNA provided the conceptual framework for analyzing adversary networks, and identifying functional roles, organizational positions, and influential actors. At the tactical level, SNA theory supported the practical need for conducting "pattern of life" analysis and developing associational links and activities matrices. This also enabled detailed network visualization by identifying key personalities, habits, locations, movement routes, and financial transactions down to the level of the individual combatant. Such information formed the basis of detailed "target information folders," a preferred method for systematically representing individual nodes in the adversary network.

The intelligence products developed from social network analysis supported HVI targeting with actionable information, including detailed physical descriptions of individual targets, biographic histories, familial relations, biometric data, cell phone numbers, and even car descriptions.[39] These methods were widely credited as being central to the tactical successes achieved during the "surge" period in 2007 when joint fusion cells applied these techniques "to locate, target and kill key individuals" within terrorist organizations, insurgent cells, and Shia militias.[40] The population-centric approaches to counterinsurgency and focused counterterrorism efforts placed "identity operations" at the center of efforts "to positively identify, track, characterize, and disrupt threat actors."[41] SNA-based targeting against high-value individuals were also leveraged against facilitation networks (finance, recruitment, training, logistics, media, command, and control) and in support of nonkinetic activities such as leaflet drops, "most wanted" posters, text messaging campaigns, and tip hotlines, all used to create a "spotlight effect" against specific threat actors.[42]

Since the end of combat operations in Iraq and Afghanistan, social network theory has matured more fully into a foundational component of doctrinal thinking, evident in the most recent versions of the Army's Operations Field Manual, the new doctrinal publication for Intelligence Analysis, the Joint Intelligence Preparation of the Operational Environment, and the Army's field manual on Targeting, among other sources.[43] SNA techniques have also become part of the military's institutional training programs and remain widely discussed in professional literature relating to the conduct of irregular and hybrid warfare, counterterrorism, and stability operations.[44]

Over the last decade as SNA techniques became more integrated into the operational targeting process, the military services (primarily the Army and Marine Corps) developed more formalized approaches to "identity operations." The Marine Corps has arguably been the most forward leaning in terms of institutionalizing these operational lessons into doctrine.[45] This strategy focuses on identifying individuals and networks seeking to disrupt operations while providing tactical commanders with "near real-time information to establish the identity, affiliations, and authorizations of an individual, to scientifically link people, places, and events, deny anonymity and freedom of movement."[46] The Marine Corps has integrated these "identity-based strategies" across the six-phase joint-campaign planning construct, reflecting the need to collect, exploit, and analyze these signatures well in advance of operations in order to reduce threat anonymity. This concept was recently codified in *U.S. Marine Corps Identity Operations* (IdOps) *Strategy 2020* that provided a holistic vision and approach for the development of IdOps across the range of military operations.[47]

The Department of Defense (DoD) has recently introduced a concept for Identity Intelligence (I2) into joint doctrine, further refining the methodology for personality-based targeting.[48] I2 is not an intelligence process per se, but rather the tailored analytical products derived from the fusion of identity attributes (biologic, biographic, behavioral, and reputational information) in the operational planning process. I2 integrates several distinct technical functional areas, including Biometrics Enabled Intelligence (BEI),

Forensics Enabled Intelligence, Document and Media Exploitation, and other all-source data for the purpose of "connecting individuals to other persons, places, events, or materials" and analyzing patterns of life.[49] This new doctrine identifies a key role for I2 across a wide range of mission areas to positively identify and distinguish specific actors on the battlefield. These include missions such as focused raids, checkpoint and area security operations, border control and maritime interdiction, force protection, support to host-nation rule of law, and analytical tasks requiring detailed "human terrain" mapping.

In sum, the security challenges of the last decade have clearly highlighted the increasing relevance of identity on the modern battlefield. This has been demonstrated in the evolution of counterterrorism targeting, as well as during counterinsurgency campaigns against irregular forces able to blend in with local populations and use anonymity for operational advantage. This mode of warfighting represents a significant departure from the doctrines of industrial-age warfare with its emphasis on large-scale maneuver, firepower, and conventional force engagement. This change has been reflected in new doctrinal approaches emphasizing tools such as SNA and IdOps into the planning and targeting process.

The new doctrines of iWar have been designed specifically to meet the challenge of combating networked adversaries and the analytical demands of a highly refined targeting process focused on the lowest common battlefield denominator—the individual combatant. As the next section highlights, these approaches would not have been possible without the concurrent development of several key technologies that have enabled U.S. forces to collect and analyze large amounts of identity information for screening and targeting individual combatants.

iWar as a Driver of Technology Innovation.

Operationalizing the doctrines of iWar depended upon the concurrent development of several enabling technologies, many of which had not been used on the battlefield prior to 9/11. These included innovations in persistent surveillance, standoff precision strike, biometrics and expeditionary forensics, and advanced analytical and information management tools designed for sharing identity data across the entire national security enterprise. These technologies helped to create an informational base layer enabling the "patient and relentless man-hunting campaign" waged by the U.S. military against networked adversaries and individual combatants.[50]

The adoption of cutting-edge technologies for the waging of iWar has largely been consistent with previous episodes of military innovation defined by a deep-seated American bias for techno-scientific approaches to strategy. Much of the intellectual genealogy for iWar can be traced back to concepts formed by post-World War II era cybernetics and the effort to apply engineering and advanced mathematical techniques to national security problems.[51] Cybernetics provided the foundational thinking for later evolutions in warfighting theory such as network-centric warfare, revolution in military affairs (RMA) technologies, and effects-based operations.[52] The use of quantitative data and advanced analytics in support of precision targeting has been the consistent theme among the evolution of these warfighting theories, including in the rise of iWar.

Similar thinking also influenced America's last experience of waging counterinsurgency during Vietnam with the application of scientific tools and quantitative methods that ultimately failed to deliver desired strategic outcomes.[53] Even amidst this failure, General William Westmoreland and others prophesized a future battlefield where:

> enemy forces will be located, tracked, and targeted almost instantaneously through the use of data links, computer assisted intelligence evaluation, and…with surveillance devices that can continually track the enemy.[54]

Such notions fed much of the thinking on military innovation during the 1970s and 1980s which focused on creating a precision strike revolution with breakthrough technologies in the areas of reconnaissance, surveillance, and target acquisition. However, this revolution was directed primarily at the operational challenges of a Cold War battlefield and conventional force engagement. These efforts sought to prove the observation of General William E. DePuy, first Commander of the Army's Training and Doctrine Command, that "what can be seen, can be hit. What can be hit, can be killed."[55]

Many of the tools developed during this period of technical innovation contributed to the stunning results during the first Gulf War. They were applied again as part of the initial approach to operations in Afghanistan and Iraq based on the presumption that "surgical" campaigns would achieve similar strategic results without requiring large ground formations and lengthy occupations. However, in both campaigns, it soon became apparent that the emergence of a new kind of adversary would require a different set of tools and methods better suited for analyzing and targeting against networks and irregular combatants. This realization marked the beginning of a process to adapt a generation of legacy tools and technologies designed for the Cold War era to the new demands of fighting small cells and individual combatants. This involved repurposing existing technologies for new tasks, as well as integrating cutting-edge capabilities such as drones, biometrics, and expeditionary forensics into operational use.

Certainly most visible among these tools has been the use of unmanned aerial vehicles, or drones. Prior to 9/11, their operational use was limited primarily to reconnaissance missions in the Balkans and Afghanistan. They were not successfully tested as a weapons platform until early-2001, then rapidly adapted to kinetic targeting in Afghanistan. Early in the campaign, General Tommy Franks called the Predator "my most capable sensor in hunting down and killing al Qaeda and Taliban leadership."[56] The inventory of these platforms increased 40-fold between 2002 and 2010, with dramatic expansion in operational use.[57] For example, during all of 2007, there was a total of 74 military drone strikes in Afghanistan; however, by 2012, that number averaged 33 strikes **per month**.[58]

Over time, a combination of improved sensors and software packages has enabled analysts to "recognize and categorize humans and human-made objects," providing unprecedented real-time surveillance and detailed granularity for tracking individual combatants.[59] Perhaps more significantly has been the degree to which targeted drone strikes "have gone from a relative rarity to a relatively common practice" as part of U.S. counterterrorism strategy.[60] The first example of this was the 2001 Predator strike that killed

Mohammed Atef, a senior al-Qaeda member linked to the 1998 U.S. embassy bombings in Tanzania and Kenya.[61] Since then, these strikes have become a key tactic used against al-Qaeda, the Taliban, and affiliated groups in Pakistan since 2007, in Yemen since 2009, and in Somalia since 2006.[62] Unclassified estimates suggest that over 98 percent of nonbattlefield targeted killings conducted by the United States over the last decade have been launched from these platforms.[63]

While drone warfare has captured the lion's share of public attention, arguably the operationalization of biometrics and expeditionary forensics offers a more vivid demonstration of how technology trends have evolved in support of individualized warfare and identity-based targeting. These innovations emerged directly from the operational challenges of counterinsurgency and the need to identify and distinguish adversaries from the larger population. This requirement led to the rapid development and use of tactical biometric systems on the battlefield in both Iraq and Afghanistan.[64]

As with drone technology, there had been no significant operational use of biometrics by the U.S. military prior to 9/11. The Army's biometric development program only began in 1999 at the Battle Command Battle Laboratory, and by 2001 had produced the first iteration of the Biometric Automated Toolset (BAT), a multi-modal (fingerprint, iris, and face) system for collecting, matching, and storing biometric and personally identifying information. The technology was initially field tested in the Balkans for identifying and tracking local national workers accessing U.S. installations; however, soon after the start of combat operations in Afghanistan and Iraq, military planners recognized the urgent need for identity management tools on the battlefield. Given early operational challenges, DoD quickly recognized biometric identification "as a basic warfighting capability, especially when fighting insurgent enemies who hide among the civilian populations."[65]

The BAT prototype was fielded to Joint Special Operations Command in Afghanistan in early-2002 for enrolling persons of interests. By 2003, it was being used in Iraq as well, first at the Abu Ghraib detention facility for detainee management and later for biometrically linking detainees to interrogation reporting.[66] BAT was also issued to Marine Corps units and used during the resettlement of Fallujah following major combat operations in 2004. As residents reentered the city, U.S. forces screened and biometrically registered all males, collecting names, birth dates, places of birth, religious affiliations, height, weight, hair and eye color, fingerprint and iris scans, and digital photographs. This data was compared against identities of known and suspected insurgents and linked to biometric identification cards that were used to monitor the flow of male residents into and out of the city.[67] A separate incident that same month in Mosul starkly demonstrated the pressing need to verify and track identities on the battlefield after a military dining facility was bombed by an insurgent with access to the base, killing 22 people. Identity management tools became an operational necessity in an environment where an anonymous enemy circulated freely just outside the gates.

The operational use of biometrics expanded rapidly as the United States shifted toward a population-central counterinsurgency strategy in Iraq and was a critical tool during the "surge" period as one of the primary means of separating insurgents from the larger population. Multi-modal or "13-point biometric" collection (10 fingers, two irises, and one face) became a standard feature of encounters with the local population during combat patrols. As the identity database grew over time, biometrics, linked with operational forensics, were used extensively for analyzing and penetrating cells employing IEDs against coalition forces. For example, during 2007-08, more than 1,700 individuals were biometrically linked to forensic evidence relating to the manufacture and use of these weapons against coalition forces.[68] The same year, information contained in biometric databases revealed that numerous Iraqi personnel applying for selection into the Iraqi Police Academy had identities matching previously-detained terrorists and insurgent suspects, and even several individuals with felony records in the United States.[69] By 2011, at the end of operations in Iraq, the United States had compiled a biometric database containing some three million files on Iraqi citizens.[70]

Similarly in Afghanistan, over 7,000 biometric collection devices were employed in support of detention operations, execution of high-risk warrants, and targeted raids against named insurgents. Between 2004 and 2011, U.S. forces made 1.6 million biometric enrollments on more than 1.1 million individuals — roughly equivalent to one of every six fighting-age males, and used this data to identify positively more than 3,000 enemy combatants.[71] This capability was particularly important in Afghanistan, a country with limited institutional capacity for identity verification; few birth certificates, drivers' licenses, or citizenship documents. This situation was exacerbated by an active black market in forged identity papers.

The integration of BEI into the targeting cycle degraded insurgent leadership capability to hide among the local population and exposed lower-level cell structures. Coalition and Afghan forces also regularly employed biometric watch lists and "be on the lookout" messages which led to the "arrests, warrants, and the removal of insurgent anonymity."[72] By the end of active combat operations in Afghanistan, the United States had placed some 33,000 individuals' identities on the biometrically enabled watch list.[73] One vivid example demonstrating the power of such information came in 2011 after some 500 Taliban prisoners escaped from Kandahar's Sarposa prison. All of the detainees had previously undergone biometric enrollment, and within 1 month, some 30 individuals were recaptured just as a result of random biometric checks in the local area.[74]

One outcome of this extensive biometric data collection on the battlefield has been an improved capability to monitor combatant identities and track cases of fighter recidivism. Estimates of recidivism rates have been somewhat variable due to the challenge of verification, classification, and how the term "reengagement" is defined; however, there is a general acknowledgment that some nontrivial portion of released and escaped detainees historically have returned to active fighting.[75] For example, toward the end of U.S. combat operations in Iraq, approximately 10 percent of all biometric matches made by forensic linkage to explosives device materials revealed an association with individuals previously released from detention. More recently, Abu Bakr al-Baghdadi, the "emir" of the Islamic State, emerged as perhaps the most famous recidivist. He was originally captured by U.S. forces in 2004 near Fallujah and later spent time in U.S. detainment facilities at Camps Bucca and Ad-der before his release. Separately, a recent Iraqi gov-ernment report estimated that some 17 of the 25 most important Islamic State leaders also spent time in U.S. facilities between 2004 and 2011.[76] Biometric tech-nologies have offered one of the few effective means of tracking this recidivism and monitoring foreign fighter flows through zones of conflict.

Since their introduction in Iraq and Afghanistan, biometric technologies have spread to other theaters with similar operational challenges of identity veri-fication, such as counterpiracy operations in East Africa.[77] As an identity intelligence specialist at the Army's Training and Doctrine Command explained, "biometrics puts a uniform on the enemy" and en-ables the categorization of actors even in the absence of traditional status-based signatures.[78] Recognizing the operational value of this technology, DoD recently designated biometrics as a core function and directed combatant commands to integrate biometrics into mission planning.[79] The U.S. Army, in particular, has continued pushing for integration of new modalities, most recently with the development of Voice Iden-tity Biometric Exploitation Services (VIBES), a tool for standoff voice identification, tracking of high-value individuals, and biometrically-enabled network link analysis.[80] Other efforts include development of new-er and more portable versions of handheld devices for biometric collection, as well as an ongoing upgrade to the Automated Biometric Identification System (ABIS) database for managing and sharing biometric data across the government.[81]

Expeditionary forensics is another area where a new military technology evolved rapidly in response to the operational demands of waging iWar. Over the last decade, forensic tools and analysis have been central to evidenced based targeting methods to "individualize, identify, associate, and scientifically link people, places, things, intentions, activities, organizations, and events." In late-2004, U.S. forces in Iraq pioneered the use of expeditionary forensics for identifying IED makers and networks. This began with the National Ground Intelligence Center expanding the existing capabilities of the Combined Explosives Exploitation Cells, primarily focused on the technical intelligence and chemical analysis of weapons.

The forward presence of these labs "greatly increased the qualitative and quantitative capacity of U.S. forces to recognize, preserve, and analyze forensic materials in-theater" and support identity-based targeting methods against insurgent networks.[82] By 2006, these facilities were employed in both Iraq and Afghanistan, including new capabilities for ammunition, clothing, latent fingerprints, and deoxyribonucleic acid (DNA) analysis, as well as digital media forensics. By 2010, the United States had deployed a total of seven such expeditionary laboratories to Iraq and eight to Afghanistan.[83] During that year alone, they enabled operational targeting and capture of over 700 high-value individuals associated with IED networks, suspected terrorists, and other criminal actors.[84]

Particularly in the case of DNA analysis, prior to Iraq and Afghanistan there was very limited operational use of this technology beyond its traditional role supporting criminal investigations. Though highly accurate, the existing technologies for DNA analysis were slow and expensive, therefore generally limited to laboratory use. This situation changed dramatically over the last decade with a focused effort by the military to modularize these capabilities into mobile labs working in direct support of operational commanders. Initially in Iraq, these were used primarily in a criminal forensics role for investigating extrajudicial killings; however, over time, the mission expanded to analysis of samples recovered from torture houses, terrorist caches, and identification of high-value individuals killed or captured during targeted raids.

By 2008, U.S. forces reportedly had gathered some 80,000 individual DNA samples in support of military law enforcement and intelligence requirements.[85] By that time, expeditionary labs were capable of processing high-priority samples in less than 24 hours.[86] Perhaps their most famous application came when a U.S. military forensics laboratory in Afghanistan analyzed DNA from Osama bin Laden's corpse to confirm his identify shortly after the raid by a U.S. Navy Sea, Air, Land team in May of 2011.[87] More recently, U.S. Special Operations forces have been field testing rapid DNA readers in forward locations, using commercial devices weighing around 60 pounds that deliver results in less than 90 minutes, a significant improvement over technologies available just a few years ago.[88]

Over the last decade, the emerging technologies supporting forensic analysis became critical to "evidence-based" targeting approaches used as part of counterterrorism and counterinsurgency strategies, as well as contributing to stability operations, local governance, and reestablishing rule of law. During the transition period from combat operations in Iraq and Afghanistan, the indigenous criminal justice system became the only means of removing insurgents and terrorists from the battlefield, and forensic science became a primary tool enabling U.S. forces to "accurately identify subjects of interest and provide irrefutable links to criminal and terrorist activities" in a manner consistent with recognized evidentiary standards.[89] For example, during 2012, U.S. forces provided forensic evidentiary analysis in support of some 120 Afghan court cases linking enemy combatants to latent fingerprints and DNA evidence, resulting in a 97 percent conviction rate in these cases.[90] As a practical matter, this also meant that targeting operations frequently were tailored for the specific purpose of obtaining evidentiary material in support of criminal proceedings and conviction under rules of civil law.[91]

One study on the use of forensics and biometrics during these campaigns noted how these technologies directly supported "precise fires to shape the operational environment, including supply chain interdiction, counterthreat finance operations, information operations, cache destruction, and the capture of high-value individuals."[92] As one example, the U.S. task force responsible for detainee operations in Afghanistan estimated that some 70 percent of individual targets captured on the battlefield were identified with the help of biometrics and forensics technologies.[93] Separately, a U.S. Government Accountability Office study concluded that the conflicts in Iraq and Afghanistan had revolutionized expeditionary forensics, specifically the use of latent fingerprints and DNA analysis in support of military operations.[94]

The rapid growth of biometrics, forensics, and large amounts of incoming data from persistent surveillance platforms all created a new challenge for analysts—specifically the task of sorting through an unprecedented amount of battlefield information gathered at the tactical level. According to one report, this deluge of sensor data was making it "nearly impossible to track and identify suspicious activities and potential security threats solely through human analytical processes."[95] A related problem was in processing and correlating multiple streams of unstructured data such as patrol reports, cell phone numbers, biographic data, document and media files, biometric signatures, and forensic evidence. The enormity of this challenge made information management a singularly critical task in the waging of iWar. For this reason, the development of new tools and methods for organizing, storing, analyzing, and disseminating this data became a major, if underappreciated, achievement of military-technical innovation over the last decade.

As U.S. forces began collecting large amounts of biometric data on the battlefield, there was an urgent need for an authoritative database to process, store, and match biometric results. This included the ability to share identity information between widely dispersed tactical forces, as well as among other DoD elements, the intelligence community, and domestic law enforcement. This led to the initial prototype design in 2004 for what would eventually become the ABIS, the military's centralized multi-modal biometric data repository which is able to process, store, and produce match results for fingerprint, palm print, iris scans, and facial scans from persons of interest. This system was designed to support a diverse range of operational functions, including detainee operations, force protection, counterterrorism screening, special operations targeting, and other intelligence requirements.[96] Importantly, it was structured for the capability to share data with other DoD, interagency, and multinational partners. Following the initial fielding of ABIS a Biometrically Enabled Watchlist feature was integrated that enabled analysts to highlight person-of-interest records and provide specific disposition instructions for each individual of interest.[97]

As DoD began collecting enormous amounts of identity data on the battlefield, there was also a need for improved processing and analytical capabilities to sort through the growing repository data and leverage SNA methodologies in support of targeting. This led to the adaptation of analytic tools such as Analyst Notebook, part of the Distributed Common Ground System, and the controversial Palantir platform used by military units in Afghanistan and elsewhere. Palantir was used for network analysis and data visualization and was based on commercial applications originally developed at PayPal for use against cybercrime networks and in detecting fraudulent financial transactions.[98] The software has also been used to analyze urban crime patterns, mapping Mexican drug cartel activity, and recently for deconstructing a Syrian suicide-bombing network by analyzing hundreds of al-Qaeda personnel records captured by U.S. forces in Iraq.[99]

With the increasing need to identify, track, and target individuals across the battlefield, other specialized tools were developed that more specifically focused on identity management and attribute correlation. One such application, the Special Operations Forces Exploitation portal, was designed for collection, transmission, and enrollment of biometric, forensic, and document and media data in support of identity discovery and analysis. Within the Army's Distributed Common Ground System architecture, the Counterintelligence and Human Intelligence Automated Reporting and Collection Systems is a platform designed for managing and analyzing identity based information derived from interrogations, biometric collection, and document exploitation operations.[100] The DoD's Biometrics Identity Intelligence Resource is another tool allowing intelligence specialists to analyze and fuse biometrics information stored within ABIS and provide this information to the users in the field. This includes a capability for correlating identity attributes with situational, contextual, and temporal data associated with biometric collection events.[101]

The evolution of these systems over the last decade highlights the central importance of information management and data analysis to the waging of iWar. While originally focused on identity verification and force protection, over time these biometric tools were adapted for direct support of targeting. Somewhat less recognized has been the degree to which these military technologies and methods have been integrated into the larger national security enterprise, in particular their contribution to the identity-based screening approaches that have become the central component of how iWar is being waged at home as well as abroad. The migration of these tools from the battlefield to the home front has been combined with an unprecedented expansion of information sharing between the military, intelligence, and domestic law enforcement communities.

The current effort of tracking and monitoring foreign fighters operating in Syria demonstrates the degree to which iWar has become a whole-of-government enterprise, dependent on data sharing, operational collaboration, and technical integration across the entire national security apparatus. This strategy has focused primarily on monitoring, interdicting, and investigating potential threats to the homeland, most notably through the screening of foreign travelers entering at border control points, but also indentification of "home grown" extremists potentially affiliated with international terrorism. As with military targeting in Iraq and Afghanistan, over the last decade these domestic security programs have become increasingly intelligence-driven, identity-based, and dependent on the use of advanced information management technologies.

This first line of homeland defense is comprised of a variety of immigration screening programs directed primarily at transportation networks and ports of entry. Identity management has become the central element of this risk-based screening process based on biographic information and biometric checks of foreign travelers seeking to enter the United States. This information is held within a network of interoperable databases that enable government agents to access biographic, biometric, and, in some cases, DNA data, held by the Departments of Justice, State, and Defense, and the intelligence community.[102] Two examples of this frontline identity-based screening architecture are the Electronic System for Travel Authorization (ESTA) and the Visitor and Immigration Status Indicator Technology (US-VISIT) Program. ESTA is a name-based biographic database used to determine traveler eligibility and screen potential risks from foreign nationals prior to entering the United States. ESTA is complimented by the US-VISIT Program that includes multiple databases of biographical and biometric data used to verify identity and cross check travelers against national-level watch lists.[103]

Many of the technologies and methods being applied against these new homeland security challenges evolved in parallel with those employed in Iraq and Afghanistan, often sharing the same data on potential threats. One notable example is the Federal Bureau of Investigation's (FBI) Next Generation Identification (NGI) system, the bureau's recently updated biometric repository containing over 100 million fingerprint records and other biometric files.[104] This system includes a facial recognition pilot project with a capability for searching criminal mug shots, as well as planned integration of palm print, iris, scars, marks, tattoos, and latent fingerprints into the searchable national database. Similarly, the Department of Homeland Security (DHS) maintains its own automated biometric identification system (IDENT), a repository of biometric and biographic data used for national security, law enforcement, immigration, and border management. IDENT supports homeland security requirements by providing iris and facial matching capabilities to the U.S. Border Patrol and other entities. According to a recent estimate, IDENT processes some 300,000 transactions per day, drawing on a database of some 173 million unique identities.[105] This database is also linked to the U.S. Coast Guard's Biometrics at Sea System program that is comprised of portable biometric systems deployed on 23 cutters used for identifying unknown individuals in the maritime environment, including suspected terrorists, criminal suspects, and other individuals of interest.[106]

The analytical power derived from this interagency data integration was recently demonstrated when the FBI identified a masked Islamic State terrorist known as "Jihadi John," who had appeared in videos depicting the killing of several hostages, including an American citizen. Based on image and voice data, the FBI reportedly identified the individual with the assistance of DoD and foreign intelligence partners. The FBI's Assistant Director for the Criminal Justice Information Services Division noted that:

> the FBI absolutely could not do its mission if we didn't have interoperability with DHS and interoperability

with DOD, because they have holdings in their bio-metric repositories . . . data that may be a piece that we don't have.[107]

Department of State and overseas consular officers also use similar biometric tools and biographic data-bases, such as the Consular Consolidated Database (CCD) for screening all U.S. visa applicants. In 2001 the CCD began storing photographs of all visa appli-cants, and since 2007 has included 10-digit biometric fingerprint scans that can be cross-referenced against data contained in the DHS, FBI, and DoD systems.[108] This database reportedly contains some 143 million biographic records of visa applications dating back to the mid-1990s.[109] As part of visa processing, consular officers are required to check applicant backgrounds against the Consular Lookout and Support System that lists individuals of concern and those who have been previously denied visas. This database contains over 42.5 million records, approximately 70 percent of which come from other agencies, including DHS, the FBI, and the Drug Enforcement Administration.[110]

All of the major defense, intelligence community, and homeland security screening programs are de-signed to leverage identity information contained in the Terrorism Screening Database that is maintained by the FBI's Terrorist Screening Center (TSC). In the first 2 years after its inauguration in 2003, the TSC re-portedly issued some 6,000 alerts to U.S. security ser-vices based on known terrorist identities or individu-als suspected of foreign terror connections.[111] A recent expansion of the architecture now enables an auto-mated review of all nonimmigrant visa applicants to identify any potential terrorism connections contained in the Terrorist Identities Datamart Environment

(TIDE) and other national databases.[112] In some cases, this also includes information obtained from foreign partners through reciprocal data sharing agreements pertaining to lost and stolen passports, reservation data, biometric information, and even DNA profiles identifying possible connections between known terrorists and unknown associates.[113]

A separate but integrated database, TIDE, is also maintained by the National Counterterrorism Center. This dataset includes all-source and classified information provided by the FBI, intelligence community, and DoD components, and has become the nation's consolidated record for screening, detection, and interdiction of known and suspected terrorists. Extracts from the TIDE are used to compile the watch lists for various domestic security programs including the Transportation Security Administration's Secure Flight program that vets passenger identities from all in-bound and outbound manifests from U.S. airports.[114] As of the beginning of 2014, TIDE contained record files on some 1.1 million individuals.[115] According to unconfirmed press reporting, the database also includes some 47,000 identities cross-listed on so-called "no-fly lists," as well as some 860,000 biometric files.[116] During the years of active combat operations in Iraq and Afghanistan, the U.S. military was the dominant contributor of biometric and identity information into the TIDE database; however, unconfirmed press reports suggests that the balance has shifted somewhat in recent years as the intelligence community and federal and local law enforcement all contribute new identity information and provide watch list nominations.[117]

Similar information architecture has also evolved around the collection and storage of DNA data. Traditionally, this data has been used to support law enforcement investigations; however, it is increasingly being applied to national security, defense, and intelligence requirements. A 2007 Defense Science Board Task Force on Biometrics described a DoD forensic counterterrorism concept evolving after 9/11 to develop "a secure repository and interactive database, which will focus on archiving, retrieving, and interpreting bio-molecular data for the identification and tracking of terrorist suspects." Within DoD, the Armed Forces DNA Identification Laboratory has maintained such a "red force" DNA database, including profiles from non-U.S. battlefield detainees, unknown DNA gathered as a result of raids, and forensic evidence collected at other sensitive sites.[118] By 2007, the Joint Federal Agencies Intelligence DNA Database reportedly contained over 15,000 DNA profiles, with twice as many samples waiting to be processed. During the years of active combat operations in Iraq and Afghanistan, DoD was the primary customer for this analysis; however, the database has also supported the intelligence community, domestic law enforcement, and FBI investigations for counter-IED efforts.[119]

The U.S. Army's Criminal Investigation Laboratory (USACIL) also provides DNA data that is entered into the FBI's Combined DNA Index System (CODIS) that allows federal, state, and local crime laboratories to store, search, and share DNA profiles electronically. As of late-2014, the FBI's CODIS database contained over 11 million offender profiles, two million arrestee profiles, and nearly 600,000 forensic profiles.[120] Internationally, some 30 countries have similar CODIS-like databases, many using compatible technical standards and formatting making it possible for profiles to be compared between national databases.[121] USACIL also supports the National DNA Index System (part of

CODIS) by providing DNA profiles of interest relating to law enforcement concerns, detainees and counter-terrorism identities. However, this database is predominantly a "blue force" repository for specimens used in mortuary affairs and criminal investigations, and not sufficiently populated with target profiles to make it tactically responsive for operational targeting. One program manager described the current process for rapid DNA as being "about where fingerprints were 10 or 12 years ago."[122]

In addition to improved data integration and analytical tools, other recent advancements have helped to make biometric and forensics technologies operationally viable over the last decade, including miniaturization and portability of collection devices. The prototype U.S. biometric system originally developed in 1999 by the Army's Battle Command Laboratory was developed principally for use at fixed facilities to manage base access in the Balkans. The original technology was not highly mobile and lacked real-time connectivity to remote servers for data transfer and watch list updates. The operational demands encountered early in Iraq led to efforts to improve miniaturization, portability, and remote connectivity as seen in subsequent iterations of the BAT and later in the Handheld Interagency Identity Detection Equipment system deployed in 2007.

Forensic science followed a similar trajectory with the development of self-contained, mobile forensics laboratories. These modular and scalable "labs-in-a-box" were designed specifically for tactical ground transport and inter-theater lift with deployed technicians to support forensic analysis at forward locations. The labs offered a full range of exploitation capabilities that were generally only available at fixed laboratory facilities prior to 9/11. These new expeditionary capabilities included analysis of latent prints, DNA, firearms and toolmarks, trace chemicals, and document and media exploitation.[123]

As these technologies demonstrated their utility for identity-based screening and targeting in Iraq and Afghanistan, they began migrating into use for domestic law enforcement, immigration, and border control functions. For example, the FBI's new biometric system has been designed to enhance connectivity down to local law enforcement authorities with mobile devices for fingerprint collection and real-time feedback on matches against the FBI's criminal database. Similarly, its Interstate Photo System now uses upgraded facial recognition technology for searching suspect photos against images for millions of known criminal identities.[124] The U.S. Customs and Border Protection specifically studied lessons learned in Iraq and Afghanistan in order to apply similar tools and methods for its identity-based screening programs and operations at remote locations along the border. This led to a program enabling mobile biometric collection to have real-time matching against national level databases of criminal and terrorist identities.[125] The agency has also begun a pilot program using new facial recognition technology for comparing passport photos with travelers' faces in order to detect illegitimate documents.[126]

In sum, over the last decade, the rise of iWar has introduced a new operational paradigm and approach to warfare characterized by three distinct elements: **individualization**, **identity**, and **information**. This transformation has been based on the systematic disaggregation of national security threats down to the lowest tactical level and a strategic prioritization on countering emerging threats from nonstate actors and individual combatants. This operational focus has driven a decade of doctrinal and technical innovation focused on identity-base screening and highly personalized forms of military targeting. This new mode of warfare rests upon a foundational layer of information technology that has enabled an unprecedented level of data collection and information sharing across the entire U.S. national security apparatus. This phenomena reflects a larger organizational dynamic closely related to the iWar paradigm, specifically how this form of warfare has led to a gradual erosion of traditional boundaries separating military operations, foreign intelligence, and domestic security functions. Additionally, as U.S. national security strategy has focused on the threats posed by individual combatants and nonstate actors, it has created the political context for perpetual warfare with few discernable geographic or temporal boundaries. The next section briefly examines the rise of iWar within the context of these policy decisions and considers the implications for the future of national security strategy.

iWar as Policy Choice.

The new doctrines and supporting technologies provided the means and methods of iWar; however, ultimately this paradigm shift resulted from policy choices and strategic decisions made in response to perceptions about a changing threat environment. The 2001 *Authorization for Use of Military Force* (AUMF) established the initial legal context for waging war against geographically dispersed networks and individuals. Using broad language, it authorizes the use of force against "nations, organizations, or **persons**."[127] Central Intelligence Agency (CIA) Director

John Brennan recently articulated how this original AUMF construct has been applied against a broad range of threats, noting that, "in this armed conflict, individuals who are part of al-Qaida or its associated forces are legitimate military targets."[128] Over time, the use of "targeted killings" against al-Qaeda leadership targets has evolved as a centerpiece of the U.S. counterterrorism approach and has been used extensively in Pakistan, Yemen, Libya, and elsewhere. However, by any estimation, this approach has expanded far deeper than limited targeting of high-level leadership figures and now represents a new mode of warfare being waged by means of "precise attacks against individuals."[129]

Arguably, the use of such focused, individualized approaches to counterterrorism has been the logical path for a liberal democracy dealing with the threat of terrorism, while also seeking to balance civil liberties in a pluralistic society. Public discomfort with profiling techniques used in the aftermath of 9/11 created political pressure for methods focused more specifically on individuals with legitimate connections to terrorism rather than categorical measures applied against entire suspect groups (racial, ethnic, religious, or otherwise). More recently, popular concern over the broad application of domestic surveillance by the National Security Agency (NSA) suggests a similar worry with dragnet-like approaches involving bulk signals collection. Nevertheless, Americans generally have expressed few reservations with focused intelligence gathering, even lethal targeting, when based on evidentiary approaches and presumptions of culpability.[130] Thus, as a matter of policy, the waging of iWar has presented few political liabilities for successive administrations.

Similar thinking seems behind the general public acquiescence over "watch listing" methods designed to screen and identify individuals with known or suspected ties to terrorism.[131] For example, the 2008 *National Security Presidential Directive 59*, authorizing biometric collection and information sharing on persons posing potential threats to national security, drew relatively little public attention.[132] Dennis C. Blair, the Director of National Intelligence, perhaps best captured the new logic of personalized risk assessment when he observed how the threat of terrorism has changed the approach to strategic warning, noting that now there are "names and faces to go with that warning."[133] In general, Americans appear somewhat resigned to such identity-based counterterrorism approaches as long as they appear directed at potential threats and not applied indiscriminately.

Perhaps ironically, foreign public opinion and diplomatic pressure has also played a role on pushing the United States toward the iWar paradigm and the need for greater discrimination and personalization of counterterrorism efforts. One noteworthy example has been the broad international condemnation of U.S. "signature strikes" directed against patterns of adversary behavior rather than specific individuals.[134] This approach closely resembles conventional targeting methods applied against formations, equipment, and facilities, where technical signatures provide generally reliable categorization of intended targets. However, the use of this technique against irregular or personnel targets has resulted in numerous incidents of misidentification and unintended civilian casualties, including the deaths of U.S. citizens and hostages.[135] Even under the best of circumstances, this mode of targeting can be inherently challenging. As one official with

Special Operations Command recently noted, "When we're trying to personally ID an individual, there is zero margin for error."[136] When these errors do occur, they often cause significant political repercussions, as the United States has experienced in Pakistan and Yemen, as well as numerous incidents during the course of military operations in Iraq and Afghanistan.[137]

In response to these pressures, the Barack Obama administration has moved toward an increased use of "personality" strikes directed against confirmed identities in order to avoid blowback from unintended causalities. This process reportedly has been formalized through the creation of a "disposition matrix," a dynamic, individualized, targeting database based on biographies, locations, associations, and operational profiles of high-value targets.[138] However, some critics maintain that even these strikes have not been precise enough at identifying targeted individuals, particularly in areas such as Pakistan and Yemen where the United States does not have significant forces or intelligence capabilities on the ground. One expert on drone warfare noted that the frequency of unintended casualties sustained during these strikes highlights the fact that that even today, "most individuals killed are not on a kill list, and the government does not know their names."[139]

Partly in response to these criticisms, the administration has even suggested a policy preference for the capture and prosecution of individual terrorism suspects, when feasible.[140] Given continuing concerns over long-term battlefield detention of irregular forces, this aspect of iWar as policy highlights the inherent tensions between traditional warfighting activities and law enforcement functions. In recent years, identity-based targeting packages have come to resemble arrest warrants more than Cold War-era targeting folders. Particularly during the later phases of operations in Iraq and Afghanistan, high-value targeting evolved toward "evidence-based" approaches, dependent upon identity verification and forensic science to support probable cause-like adjudications and actionable intelligence. One observer noted how the F3EAD process gradually evolved into a "police-like investigate, arrest, and convict" mode of nonlethal targeting.[141] Particularly as counterinsurgency strategy gained momentum, observers noted how soldiers on patrol began to "behave almost like city cops," doing "biometric scans and turning in evidence bags with each detainee."[142] These examples seem to support speculation by Harvard scholar Gabriella Blum that the individualization of warfare may utterly transform the nature of armed conflict, moving it more toward a policing model with greater focus on individual harms, individual victims, and individual culpability.[143]

From a policy perspective, the targeting paradigm of iWar has also created a challenge for strategic assessment and useful measures of effectiveness. During the history of modern warfare, a variety of measures have been applied as proxies for evaluating different operational approaches, warfighting theories, and strategic decisions. World War II offered a relatively straightforward quantitative template supported by an endless supply of statistics on the numbers of bombs dropped, convoys and factories destroyed, square miles of territory seized, soldiers captured, and units defeated on the battlefield. Such measures were well suited to an industrial-age conflict where the central strategic challenges often concerned issues of time, distance, and production—all problems generally reducible to structured analysis and quantitative assessment.[144] Conversely, Vietnam produced a perversion of such measures, particularly as enemy body counts emerged as a proxy measure for operational success in the absence of a clear political-military end state.

The iWar paradigm has replaced generic body counts of Vietnam with a modified version of effects-based assessment based on highly relativistic impact analysis. Various approaches have weighed factors such as an individual fighter's operational profile, unique technical skills, network centrality, and an actor's influence within the larger organizational network. These techniques have deep conceptual grounding in Social Network Analysis theory; however, they still rely on highly subjective measures that are difficult to apply as a centerpiece of campaign assessment. For example, one phenomena that emerged early in the Iraq war was the infamous "personality identification playing cards" issued to U.S. troops that depicted high-ranking members of Saddam Hussein's government and senior Ba'ath Party members. The cards soon developed into something of an informal yardstick for operational progress on the battlefield as key leaders were killed or captured. Attention remained focused on such measures, even as it became abundantly clear that they had no particular relevance to the evolving security dynamics on the ground.[145] Over time, similar methods have evolved for measuring the effects of counterterrorism strikes against adversary networks, applying qualitative assessments to gauge the operational impact of killing or capturing specific "high-value individuals." However, as with the body counts of Vietnam, there is an inherent artifice imbedded into the process. No matter how many times the "al-Shabaab number two" is killed, there may always be another "al-Shabaab number two." Conversely, Berlin fell only once.

The issue of operational assessment raises a larger issue in terms of evaluating the iWar paradigm both as policy choice and as a component of military strategy. While there is little debate as to the awe-inspiring tactical efficiency of U.S. techniques for identifying and targeting individual combatants on the battlefield, what is less certain is whether these methods aggregate into effective strategies for achieving larger political objectives. The perpetual regeneration of terrorist threats inside Pakistan, Yemen, and Somalia offers little evidence that identity-based targeting has been fully successful as a centerpiece of counterterrorism strategy. Likewise, the deteriorating conditions in Iraq and Afghanistan suggest limits as to what these approaches can deliver as a major component of counterinsurgency. Conversely, one can make a strong claim that the combination of these techniques has contributed, in part or whole, to protect the homeland successfully from a major terrorist attack since 9/11 by identifying and dissuading individual threats and disrupting their networks. The inherent ambiguity in the data raises the more difficult question as to whether one can evaluate effectively the utility of specific tactics and tools separately from the overall strategic outcomes they produce. As H. R. McMaster, Director of the Army's Capabilities and Integration Center, recently cautioned, "Targeting does not equal strategy."[146]

President Obama observed during a recent address to the National Defense University that "We must define the nature and scope of this struggle, or else it will define us."[147] Indeed, this has largely been the case for the U.S. national security establishment since 9/11. Over the last 15 years, these bureaucracies have undergone a revolution in form, function, and focus that has moved them toward a model of warfare far different from that of the Cold War era. These entities have developed new doctrines, technologies, and analytical methods that reflect a significant reorientation of national security priorities based on the task of defeating networked adversaries and targeting individual combatants. As one senior U.S. officer recently noted, the task of "putting warheads to foreheads" has become a core military function and arguably the reflection of a new model of state security centered on defeating threats from nonstate actors, networked adversaries, and individual combatants.

By all indications, some form of iWar will persist as a model of state security and American warfare into the future. Contemporary security challenges are likely to be characterized by operations in areas of poor governance with weak identity regimes, and against adversaries determined to use anonymity to operational advantage. Meanwhile, threats from transnational terrorists show little sign of abating. For these reasons, the operational relevance of identity on the modern battlefield and along the borders will only grow in importance.

iWar as Case Study of Military Innovation.

The rise of iWar offers a useful case study of military innovation. The iWar paradigm evolved as the result of a very specific national security challenge encountered after 9/11. Much of this doctrinal and technical innovation centered on the pressing need to identify, screen, and target individual combatants fighting as part of distributed networks. Initially, this task represented an operational challenge for which the U.S. national security apparatus was largely unprepared. Cold War-era doctrines and technologies were not conceived for the task of differentiating among individual combatants, or the challenge of screening and targeting them based on discrete identity attributes. Nor were pre-9/11 bureaucracies and warfighting strategies optimized to function across an unbounded battle space and against threats whose tactics did not conform to a clear differentiation between foreign military operations and domestic security functions. In this sense, the rise of iWar serves as a useful example for examining wartime innovation.

Scholars of military innovation generally look to several characteristics for evidence of substantive change. The first is that the process of innovation alters the manner in which military formations function in the field. The second is that these changes are significant in terms of scope and organizational impact. The third is that these reforms ultimately produce greater military effectiveness.[148] By this standard, the rise of iWar has largely satisfied the first two elements; however, the third remains open to debate, depending on the scope of analysis and terms of measure. A separate but related question is whether iWar truly represents a new operational paradigm or simply a repackaging of old ideas implemented with new technologies. Arguably, one may identify iWar precursor elements in examples such as the CIA's Phoenix Program in Vietnam and, more recently, with Israeli targeting methods used in Gaza and Lebanon. As with iWar, these examples also involved operational approaches based on network-centric analysis and highly focused, individualized targeting methods; however, several important aspects have arguably made the recent U.S. experience *sui generis*.

Foremost among these differences has been the scope of application. Operations of the iWar paradigm have taken place on a global scale, enabled by a dramatic bureaucratic transformation that has integrated military operations, foreign intelligence activities, and domestic security functions more than any other time in American history. This strategy was based on an assortment of new technical innovations virtually unknown on the battlefield prior to 9/11, including drones, biometrics, expeditionary forensics, DNA analysis, and advanced information management tools, to name just a few. The application of these tools reflected a shift toward an information-centric view of warfare far different from the conventional force paradigm of the Cold War era. This transformation included an evolution in warfighting theory that introduced new methods into the doctrinal cannon such as Social Network Analysis and personality-based targeting. All of these changes were centered on a fundamentally altered strategic logic that prioritized nonstate actors and individual combatants equally with the threats posed by state actors in the formation of national security policy. These changes also represented a subtle but profound shift in thinking about how military force should be applied against such threats, and in doing so, redefined the role of identity in modern warfare.

In analyzing these changes, some scholars suggest that the process of wartime innovation should be examined as a phenomena distinct from that of peacetime change.[149] Arguably, the causal pathways of wartime innovation tend to be somewhat less complex as they are highly responsive to exigent circumstances. This is partly due to the fact that active conflict offers a laboratory for "natural experiments" where warfighting requirements are articulated explicitly in response to the actions of an immediate adversary rather than a hypothetical one. This situation provides a crucible for immediate tactical feedback, thus creating a powerful dynamic for iterative design and rapid process improvement. These factors have the effect of sharpening how operational needs are defined and speeding the bureaucratic process of research, development, prototyping, and employment. However, rapid institutional change still requires an initial intellectual catalyst to serve as a conceptual driver to frame the strategy of innovation. Without some coherent idea that provides a common intellectual framework, the sum of innovation will inevitably be less than its parts.

In the case of iWar, this central idea was the realization that fighting against networks and individuals required an entirely different approach and toolset than methods optimized for conventional conflict. Once this overarching conceptual framework was established, the process of military innovation occurred rapidly across multiple spheres. The first sphere involved changes to warfighting theory that were translated into doctrinal design and higher-level concepts of operation. The second sphere involved the adoption of specialized technical tools and methods directly applied to tactical problems to create battlefield effects. A third sphere was a slower process of changing organizational behaviors, institutional values, and philosophical ideas about how a military service conceives of its role and defining functions within the larger national security enterprise.

At this point, iWar as an operational paradigm is at a crossroads. The challenge ahead will be to identify what aspects of the model remain relevant to future security challenges and overall U.S. defense priorities. This requires evaluating the lessons learned from the previous decade, developing supporting doctrines and technologies, establishing priorities for training, and then building the institutional foundations to support the desired capabilities. One of the most challenging aspects of this task is picking the correct technologies in the absence of a persistent operational challenge from a clearly defined adversary.

Inevitably, as the dynamics and imperatives of "peacetime" innovation take precedent, they will differ from those of wartime innovation. Other priorities are likely to grow in influence and consequently shape the debates over warfighting theory, doctrinal development, procurement strategies, and institutional roles. In the case of iWar, the United States will need to retain some of the tools and methods specialized for the purpose of differentiating friend from foe and combating networked adversaries. There is no hint that the threats from nonstate actors will soon subside, nor will the threat of "hybrid conflicts" where combatants fight without uniforms and conventional formations. The United States is also likely to conduct operations within environments characterized by weak or nonexistent identity regimes. Many of these challenges will continue to demand a place for the tools and methods of iWar.

With this reality in mind, the next section examines the emerging technology landscape and attempts to identify some of the general trends that are likely to shape how iWar will be waged in the next generation. Many of these tools have already demonstrated their utility on the battlefield and in securing the border, including biometrics, forensics, information management technology, and data analysis. These areas will continue to evolve and are likely to be enhanced by innovations in other areas, including new biometric modalities, improved DNA forensics, cyber tools and social media exploitation, advanced video and data analytics, machine learning, and computational analysis, among others.

This task of predicting technology futures is fraught with hazard. Estimations of what tools may emerge, how they will be used, and the implications of their use will inevitably appear naive in hindsight. Nevertheless, such speculation is a necessary risk for the strategist and planner who must allocate today's resources based on reasoned expectations of what may happen tomorrow. For this reason, the next section of this study introduces several emerging technology areas through a hypothetical iWar scenario involving a suspected foreign fighter. While the details and events are fictionalized, the vignette represents a realistic security dilemma for the age of iWar and addresses the continuing challenge of identifying, screening and targeting individual adversaries determined to use anonymity to operational advantage. (See Chart 1.)

	Industrial Warfare	iWar
Political Context	Westphalian; professional armies fighting as political proxies for defined geopolitical objectives; recognizes *jus in bello* constructs.	Extra-Westphalian; individual combatants fighting for ideological causes and ambiguous objectives; challenges *jus in bello* constructs.
Adversary Characteristics	State armies comprised of "generic" professional soldiers using doctrinal organized formations and functioning by depersonalized, bureaucratic logic.	Nonstate entities and "unprivileged" combatants using anonymity for operational advantage; use idiosyncratic tactics and organized by highly personalized networks.

Chart 1. Industrial Warfare versus iWar.

	Industrial Warfare	iWar
Operational Environment	Contested primarily in the physical domains (land, sea, air) and waged in a contiguous linear battle space; defined by clear operational boundaries, fire and maneuver over geographic terrain.	Contested primarily in the informational domain (influence, identity, human terrain); spatially and temporally unbounded; defined by a merger of external and domestic security spheres of concern.
Theories of Warfighting	Influenced by tenets of maneuver warfare: mass, firepower, destruction of enemy forces, and seizure of key terrain. Focus is on the operational level of war.	Influenced by counterinsurgency and counterterrorism doctrines: population-centric measures and law enforcement-like methods. Merges tactical and strategic levels of war.
Analytical Approach and Tools	Order of Battle analysis and indications and warnings (I&W) methods, platform-centric doctrinal templating, conventional Military Intel analytical models, technical signatures and intelligence, surveillance, and reconnaissance (ISR).	Social Network Analysis, Attack the Network, Identity Intelligence (I2), law enforcement analytical model, biometric and forensic signatures, document and media exploitation.
Targeting Paradigm	Status-based targeting against units, formations and equipment; Well-defined, rules-based rules of engagement (ROE).	Identity-based targeting against individuals, cells, and networks; Ambiguous, evidence-based ROE.

Chart 1. Industrial Warfare versus iWar. (cont.)

	Industrial Warfare	iWar
Objectives and Measures of Effectiveness (MOE)	Attrition and physical destruction of the adversary's war-fighting capabilities; quantitative assessment - units destroyed and terrain seized. MOE based on technical Battle Damage Assessment.	Attrition of key leadership, nodes, and specialized operators; qualitative assessment—kill/capture of High-Value Individuals. MOE based on SNA theories of network centrality, influence, and organizational cohesion.
Success Criteria and End State	Primary focus on defeat of adversary military forces, political capitulation, and the orderly demobilization and repatriation of detained combatants.	Primary focus on risk mitigation rather than military victory; no political settlement, legal limbo for detained combatants, and enduring problems of fighter recidivism.

Chart 1. Industrial Warfare versus iWar. (cont.)

THE FUTURE OF IWAR

Many of the catalysts giving rise to the iWar paradigm reflect persistent trends that are unlikely to abate in the immediate future. From a policy perspective, there is reason to expect some continuation of approaches based on the persistent monitoring of individual threats, identity-based screening, and, when necessary, personality-based targeting. The use of such methods remains relatively uncontroversial from a political perspective, and President Obama has made clear his vision of a counterterrorism strategy designed as a "surgical, precise response to a very specific problem."[150] Another important trend that is likely to remain constant is the value of anonymity as an operational enabler for many U.S. adversaries. Recent conflicts in Syria, Ukraine, and elsewhere have vividly highlighted this fact. As one commentator recently noted, in modern warfare, "Knowing the name of the person on the other-side of the battlefield is rising as a strategic necessity."[151]

The next section examines in greater detail several of the factors likely to reinforce the central pillars of the iWar paradigm. These include characteristics of the threat environment, emerging technology trends, and the changing meaning of identity.

iWar and the Threat Environment.

Several persistent trends in the contemporary threat environment appear likely to amplify many of the original catalysts that gave rise to the iWar paradigm. Recently, General McMaster described the transition from a Cold War model where nations were the primary source of threats, in contrast to today's threats:

> from nonstate actors and the confluence of networked insurgent and terrorist organizations bridging over into transnational organized crime networks and having access to capabilities they didn't have in the past.[152]

These threats include an increased potential for hybrid conflicts where conventional status-based targeting methods may not easily apply, as well as a wide range of adversaries determined to leverage anonymity for operational advantage.

The National Intelligence Council *Global Trends* report recently described a near-future security environment dominated by various forms of irregular warfare — terrorism, subversion, sabotage, insurgency, and criminal activities.[153] Testimony by the Director of the National Counterterrorism Center noted that these networks have actually grown more dangerous over time due to the erosion of central governance, making them "more geographically diffuse and involving a greater diversity of actors," thus making them an increasingly adaptive and complex threat.[154] Robert Cardillo, head of the National Geospatial-Intelligence Agency, recently observed that such groups and individuals are operating "literally without geographic bounds," thus less vulnerable to conventional military targeting methods.[155]

There has also been an apparent shift in terrorism tactics away from infrequent but spectacular operations toward a pattern of smaller, more distributed attacks often emanating from self-radicalized individuals and small groups operating independent of centralized direction. The *Global Trends* report suggested that these:

> individuals and small groups will have greater access to lethal and disruptive technologies enabling them to perpetrate large-scale violence — a capability formerly the monopoly of states.[156]

The challenge of defending against such diverse threats is likely to reinforce the key aspects of iWar, particularly U.S. reliance on technical collection, identity-based screening, and targeting efforts focused against individual actors, small cells, and networks. This includes an immediate challenge arising from the issue of foreign fighters.

The current Syrian situation exemplifies the enormous scale of the foreign fighter problem, exacerbated by relatively easy cross-border mobility and aggressive social media recruiting. According to recent estimates, as many as 20,000 foreign fighters from some 90 countries have joined various factions fighting in Syria, including thousands of European passport holders and several hundred from the United States. The head of the National Counterterrorism Center recently called the foreign fighter flow to Syria "unprecedented," at a rate far exceeding the movement of foreigners traveling to Afghanistan, Pakistan, Iraq, Yemen, or Somalia at any point over the past 20 years.[157]

Outside the United States, most countries have instituted little more than piecemeal strategies for monitoring and tracking foreign fighter flow down to the level of the individual combatant. For example, the European Union (EU) still does not have a systemic process in place for identity checks of all citizens reentering the region from abroad. During 2013 alone, Turkey denied entry to some 4,000 people listed in a no-entry database and detained another 92,000 people on its border; however, this has done little to stem the tide.[158] One recent United Nations (UN) report noted that the "slow exchange of information and data on foreign fighters is one of the major obstacles to international counterterrorism cooperation," estimating that "less than 10 percent of basic identifying information on such individuals has been entered into global multilateral databases."[159] That means that there is little, if any, timely operational information available concerning identity, travel routes, photographs, and international search warrants on individuals traveling to take part in hostilities. There has been a similar challenge with obtaining physical evidence of foreign fighter activities occurring while inside the conflict zone, making it difficult to pursue prosecution as an option or generate additional intelligence leads.[160] One U.S. senior intelligence official working on the Syrian foreign fighter problem recently described the challenge as a "decadal" issue of concern for the intelligence community.[161]

In the aftermath of the January 2015 Paris attacks, it became clear that European intelligence agencies had far too many leads to follow, too many returning foreign fighters to monitor, and not enough manpower for all of the required tasks.[162] Unfortunately, few, if any, countries possess the resources required for monitoring large numbers of suspect individuals through traditional surveillance methods. Some estimates place the cost of full-scale, round-the-clock, conventional surveillance against a single individual as high as $8 million a year.[163] Even a fraction of this cost represents an unsustainable outlay set against potentially thousands of foreign fighters expected to return home eventually from conflicts such as in Syria.

This reality inevitably will lead western governments to rely upon some combination of two approaches. First, they will expand the use of technical surveillance and screening measures aimed at gathering more information with fewer resources. Second, they will develop improved methods of risk analysis and perhaps apply predictive interventions against suspect individuals. Either of these approaches will tend to reinforce the key elements of the iWar paradigm as security threats must still be identified, monitored, and targeted with timely and accurate information. A variation of the iWar paradigm has already been proposed in France where lawmakers recently approved an unprecedented overhaul of domestic surveillance practices, now allowing for collection and analysis of telephone and internet metadata as one means of identifying potential threats posed by domestic extremists.[164]

Beyond threats from international terrorism, many security analysts have highlighted the growing risk of "hybrid conflicts" where state-based militaries attempt to obscure operational attribution by employing proxies and irregular tactics, such as with Russia's use of "little green men" in Ukraine.[165] A recent report by the International Institute for Strategic Studies highlighted the possibility of nonstate actors also employing such mixed tactics to achieve asymmetric advantage against conventional adversaries.[166] The Islamic State has demonstrated such a hybrid approach by employing a high-low mixture of conventional maneuver, insurgent-like tactics, and terrorism to achieve gains in Syria and Iraq. French forces in Mali have experienced similar challenges in waging a conventional military campaign against an "invisible enemy" where it has been difficult to "distinguish between the trafficker, the terrorist, and the rebel."[167] Even future challenges from peer competitor state militaries are likely to circumvent the significant U.S. advantage in conventional warfare by employing techniques that avoid direct confrontation and veil operational attribution. One commentator on defense technology recently observed that "war is changing, whether it is waged by emergent groups like the Islamic State or nations like Russia, more and more, the potential revelation of identity is becoming a liability in conflict zones."[168]

The expanse of U.S. global security interests also suggests continuing involvement in activities other than high-intensity conventional warfare, such as stability operations, anti-piracy, and counterillicit trafficking.[169] These tasks share several common characteristics. First, they represent activities dominated by networked adversaries, disbursed cells, and individual actors using anonymity for operational advantage. Second, such missions are likely to occur in areas characterized by weak governance and ineffective identity regimes where a significant portion of the population lacks formal documentation and verifiable identity. Such environments are notorious generators of corruption, insecurity, and instability — issues that cannot easily be contained through strategies of conventional military deterrence.

The challenge of conducting operations under weak identity regimes is generally underappreciated as a military planning factor. This may be due, in part, to the fact that many residents of the developed world take for granted the basic identity management functions of the modern state bureaucracy. This structure begins with foundational identity documents such as birth certificates then expands through one's lifetime within a system of de facto credentialing, sanctioned by the state, that are required for full participation in civic and economic life. Yet, even this most basic function of governance is absent in much of the world. According to one recent estimate, as many as 40 percent of children in the developing world do not have any kind of official identity registration generated at birth. This situation creates an initial "identity gap" that becomes prone to inaccuracies, corruption, and disenfranchisement throughout an individual's lifetime.[170]

The operational significance of identity is not only a concern for counterterrorism and insurgency, but also in peacekeeping and humanitarian relief missions. In 2014, the UN High Commission for Refugees (UNHCR) launched its first biometric pilot program in Malawi to improve security protections and better target assistance for forcibly displaced persons.[171] This program was recently expanded to the Democratic Republic of Congo in an effort to identify and register some 245,000 Rwandan refugees living in the region and 19 refugee camps in Chad where 450,000 individuals will be biometrically enrolled. UNHCR will update records using remote connections to a central biometric database maintained in Geneva, Switzerland.[172] In another example, the Turkish Disaster and Emergency Management Authority recently conducted biometric registration of 740,000 Syrian refugees displaced by fighting across the border.[173] Such identity management tools are likely to become the norm in future relief operations and humanitarian interventions in these environments.

iWar and the Technology Environment.

The changing technology environment is another factor that is likely to transform significantly the relationship between security, identity, and warfare. National security scholar Rosa Brooks recently posed the question of how warfare will be changed in an age when we increasingly know our enemy by name, by face, and even DNA. She observes that, in recent conflicts, the United States often knows a great deal about their adversaries, "between human informants and high-tech surveillance, we often know where our targets were born, where they went to school and college, the names of their siblings and children, their favorite pastimes, and much more."[174] Brooks and others like military-legal scholar Charles Dunlap have even speculated on the not-too-distant future where ultra-precise weapons armed with advanced facial recognition software will "roam battlefields looking for very specific members of an enemy's force."[175] While this scenario may not yet be reality, several information technology trends are already pushing iWar in this direction.

The next decade is likely to be remembered as the era when biometric technologies became normalized and integrated into nearly every facet of daily life. The defense, security, and law enforcement sectors were the first to recognize the value of biometrics for applications such as border control, systems access, and identity verification. These requirements largely defined the initial focus of research and development in the field, as well as how these tools evolved; however, this dynamic is rapidly changing. Private industry is already racing ahead of governments in the use of biometric technologies, particularly in the areas of personal consumer electronics and information security tools.[176] The implication is that governments increasingly are likely to trail behind in terms of influencing the direction of innovation. Industry experts have expressed concerns that a lack of proper planning and coordination among governmental agencies, and between international partners, will further diminish the role that governments play in defining the future of the industry.[177] New technical breakthroughs are likely to emerge from demand in the commercial sector, only later to be exploited by defense and security interests. In some cases, this reactive position will apply to matters of governance and rule setting, particularly as technology innovation outpaces the state's ability to define the context of its use.

This situation is a dramatic reversal of the Cold War era paradigm in which the most advanced sensors and intelligence collection platforms evolved behind the wall of protected government-sponsored research and development. This has several important implications. First, in some technical areas of iWar, the United States will find itself in a situation of technological parity with potential adversaries, whether state actors or otherwise. Second, in order to reduce the technology gap, the U.S. Government will need to resolve many long-standing deficiencies in the acquisition process in order to remain near the leading edge as new technologies evolve. Biometrics is one area in particular where this dynamic is almost certain to be the case.

One industry research organization predicts that, by the end of 2015, there will be some 619 million people using biometrics on their mobile devices, including fingerprint, voice, iris, facial, and various modalities of behavioral biometrics.[178] Other estimates suggest that over a billion people in developing countries have already registered some form of biometric signature through their interface with consumer electronic devices, financial institutions, and local governments.[179] Additionally, the inherent weaknesses of traditional methods for personal authentication (e.g., passwords) are driving significant growth from the commercial sector for improved methods of identity management.

Beyond these commercial applications, dozens of governments are pursuing biometrically enabled identification (ID) projects for e-passports and visas, voter registries, public sector payroll, health care, and social service delivery programs. Many of these initiatives are originating in the developing world where some governments have entirely bypassed a paper-based identity system and moved directly to biometrically enabled technologies. Notably, India, with a massive undocumented population, is currently in a multiyear process of biometrically registering all one billion residents as part of a new national identification system. Biometric attributes will be linked to a unique identity number and used for such functions as managing government benefits and monitoring distribution of food rations.[180]

As another example, the United Kingdom (UK) Home Office recently introduced a "biometric residence permit" that will be required for any foreign nationals from outside the European Economic Area who wish to work or study in the UK. The cardholder must present these credentials at the border when travelling into or out of the UK.[181] Other novel applications are emerging each day such as Kenya's use of biometric cards to ensure public servants show up to work and Nigeria's recent legislation mandating biometric registration of mobile phone Subscriber Identity Module (SIM) cards so the government can better track illicit activities.[182] Pakistan recently followed suit in requiring biometrically registered SIM cards after it was discovered that all six assailants in the major December 2014 attack on a Peshawar military school were using cell phones registered to a single woman with no obvious connection to the attackers.[183]

The rapid pace of innovation in the field is certain to raise concerns over privacy and surveillance. Additionally, there are likely to be challenging issues with regulatory and governance concerns as well as conflicts over technical standards, interoperability, and data integration. Perhaps most significantly, much of the development in this area is likely to evolve outside of explicit state control. Governments, security services, and militaries may find themselves in the position of being rule-takers rather than rule-makers when it comes to defining how this technology proliferates and is used by the general public. Biometrics is just one example of this general trend concerning technology innovation in the age of iWar. A similar dynamic applies to the cyber domain as well.

In recent conflicts anonymity has become an increasingly important center of gravity for nonstate actors, and, in some cases, for state actors attempting to avoid operational attribution. Protected identities can provide these adversaries with flexibility, mobility, and the advantage of surprise. Anonymity also allows for safety in communication, recruitment, financing, and planning, as well as a form of concealment from which to wage information warfare. The cyber domain offers adversaries a zone of relative sanctuary where real identities can be protected, concealed, or manipulated. Actors can conceal activities behind strong encryption, digital avatars, or technical tools that complicate attribution and thwart surveillance.

DoD's recently updated cyber strategy explicitly noted how anonymity on the web is directly enabling malicious cyber activity by state and nonstate groups. The Islamic States in Iraq and Syria (ISIS) has been one of the more notable examples of this trend. Another has been Russia's use of Internet "trolls" for generating pro-regime propaganda aimed at influencing the information environment concerning operations in the Ukraine. One recent study detailed how these anonymous "trolls" are expected to post 50 news articles daily, maintain multiple Facebook and Twitter accounts, and generate dozens of posts per day, amounting to some 40,000 online comments each day in support of pro-Kremlin information operations.[184] In recognition of these new challenges, the DoD Cyber Strategy specifically calls for "intelligence and attribution capabilities help to unmask an actor's cyber persona, identify the attack's point of origin, and determine tactics, techniques, and procedures" in order to support credible deterrence, response, and denial operations.[185]

Estonian President Toomas Hendrik Ilves has been a leading thinker on cyber defense issues and recently noted how organized crime, terrorist networks, and state actors are rapidly converging into this space, making it increasingly difficult for legitimate actors to distinguish between them.[186] The challenge of identity and attribution in the cyber domain has made it a virtual battleground for "phase zero" operations, those activities designed to shape perceptions and influence behavior as a precursor to kinetic action. Recent examples were seen prior to Russian military interventions in both Georgia and Ukraine. More broadly, the cyber domain offers a venue for influencing behavior and shaping outcomes through activities short of conventional military engagement. This approach entails fewer physical risks for adversaries by offering a greater ability to mask identities through readily available technical tools. These characteristics are making cyberspace a highly contested terrain in the age of iWar. Many of the enabling technologies in this domain are democratic and highly scalable, meaning that, unlike the most powerful weapons of the Cold War era, cyberspace weapons are generally accessible to anyone with the requisite skills and basic tools. For this reason, cyber presents the logical platform for nonstate actors seeking to employ asymmetric capabilities against states while avoiding direct attribution.

A variety of easily accessible tools can offer users parallel networks that are encrypted, decentralized, and, to some degree, anonymous. Silk Road, an online "dark web" trading site recently shut down by the

FBI is one example. Other actors rely on tools, such as the Tor network, that offer protections against traffic analysis and surveillance by masking Internet protocol (IP) addresses and server locations while encrypting data packets and routing them through multiple nodes, making it difficult to track and identify users. Some experts estimate that such dark web sites represent a significant portion of web activity, involving content generally not indexed and undiscoverable by conventional search engines such as Google.[187] In addition, digital "crypto-currencies" such as Bitcoin can provide a means for conducting pseudonymous financial transactions across these networks.[188] This architecture of anonymity enables users to browse, communicate, and trade illicit materials with a generally lower risk of detection and greater ability to conceal physical locations and identity.[189]

There is already some suggestion that the Islamic State and other extremist groups are using such methods. The head of the U.S. Treasury Department's Financial Crimes Enforcement Network recently observed that, "when you start talking about global point-to-point transactions and pseudonymity and instantaneous movement of value over borders, that has real risks associated with it."[190] Director of the NSA Admiral Michael Rogers more clearly articulated these risks, noting that as his agency monitors threats on the dark web it spends "a lot of time tracking people that can't be found."[191]

The use of the anonymous "dark web" sites is particularly striking in contrast to the concurrent rise of social media, a phenomena conceptually based on the opposite goal — specifically the projection of identity for the explicit purpose of building network connections based on attributional affiliation. Par-

72

ticularly since the Arab Spring protests, social media has played a central role in how nonstate actors craft and project their identities outward to a global audience. For many groups, social media platforms have become the preferred tool for distributed communication, planning, recruitment, and the dissemination of propaganda, including terrorist groups, insurgents, and criminal organizations. The National Intelligence Council *Global Trends* report recently described these social networking technologies as "inherently resistant to centralized oversight and control," with the potential to displace traditional power sources and authorities in favor of individuals, small groups, and ad hoc coalitions of nonstate actors.[192]

Several recent examples demonstrate the degree to which social media has evolved as an operational tool. Militant groups in Gaza, terrorist cells in Mali, oil traffickers in Nigeria, and pirates off the Somalia coast have all employed social media as ad hoc command and control networks for conducting information operations. The Islamic State, in particular, has crafted a robust and sophisticated digital presence, "disseminating timely, high-quality media content across multiple platforms."[193] A recent report on terrorism and new media found that some 90 percent of terrorist activities taking place online use social media as a networking tool, in some cases offering "a virtual firewall to help safeguard the identities of those who participate."[194] The director of Great Britain's NSA counterpart, the Government Communications Headquarters (GCHQ), recently described Twitter, Facebook, and WhatsApp as the "command-and-control networks of choice for terrorists and criminals."[195] One commentator on military technology even suggested that situational awareness in the cyber age will soon mean using "instantaneous data from social networks like Twitter and Facebook to identify the target in the sniper scope."[196] While perhaps an exaggeration, the comment does suggest the degree to which these platforms have become an important component of the contemporary operational environment.

Perhaps the Syrian conflict provides the most powerful example of how social media has become a tool of modern warfare. This conflict has been called "the most socially mediated civil conflict in history," with fighters using Facebook, YouTube, Twitter, Diaspora, and Snapchat for a variety of operational,communication, and propaganda functions.[197] For example, the Al-Nusra Front has used social media for posting press releases and informal communiqués including text, photographs, and videos detailing the fighting, and even personalized eulogies for its members killed in combat.[198] Analysis from late-2014 identified at least 46,000 Twitter accounts being used by members and supporters of the Islamic State, while the FBI estimates that some 200,000 people around the world are accessing "terrorist messaging" each day via social media, videos, instruction manuals, and other material posted on militant Islamist sites.[199]

These platforms have also been used extensively for dissemination of operational information, recruiting, and training purposes.[200] For example, sites have posted information on use of explosives, fighting techniques, and links to encryption programs designed to help users protect sensitive communications. Individual fighters are also using personal accounts to establish their bona fides and document their combat experiences first hand. In a telling example, one young British fighter attempted to fake his own battlefield death on social media after being placed on a travel watch list.[201] Eventually he was caught when attempting to enter back into the UK; however, the example highlights the degree to which many nonstate actors are leveraging social media to craft and project identities to an external audience.

However, online activism can be a double-edged sword, both enabling adversary operations, while at the same time potentially exposing them to observation and attribution. In recent years, social media exploitation and open source digital forensics have offered invaluable insights into adversary operations. For example, in early-2014 analysts were able to track Russian military personnel movements into Crimea through social media "bread crumbs" dropped by personnel preparing for mobilization. Separately, YouTube videos and Twitter messages posted by Russian irregulars provided the first hints of responsibility for the downing of Malaysia Airlines Flight 17 in eastern Ukraine in July 2014.[202] More recently, "crowd-sourced" information posted to social media by local residents has substantiated Russia's active role in eastern Ukraine, including the steady flow of weapons and troops, even as the government continues to deny any direct involvement in hostilities.[203]

In Syria, pro-Assad forces reportedly used fake online avatars to identify and target opposition members. They used these fictitious identities to obtain detailed personal information, including names and locations of opposition members, media activists, humanitarian aid workers, and others deemed dangerous to the regime.[204] These Skype accounts, mobile applications (apps), and social media sites revealed address books, records of short message service messages, email, and other information relating to opposition force campaign plans. According to one assessment, this type of aggressive social media exploitation has produced "actionable military intelligence for an immediate battlefield advantage," including information enabling pro-Assad forces to identify, track, and target key opposition members.[205]

The United States reportedly has also made use of social media data for targeting. One military official recently revealed that social media posts recently had been used to track and subsequently strike an Islamic State group headquarters building.[206] Other researchers have used social media as a means of building demographic profiles of Islamic State fighters and other groups, shedding light on their locations, what languages they speak, how they access the Internet, and for content analysis of their communications.[207] In another twist, the online international network of "hacktivist entities," known as *Anonymous*, recently took control of dozens of Twitter and Facebook accounts used by the Islamic State and threatened the group's members, promising "we will hunt you, take down your sites, accounts, emails, and expose you. . . . From now on, no safe place for you online."[208] According to one expert, such "network exploitation is now a routine part of even the most low-tech, if brutal, civil wars, and available to those operating on a shoestring budget."[209]

The information density of the cyber domain clearly presents liabilities for the "non-OPSEC [operations security] aware" foreign fighter community as posts and communications provide a window into identities and activities.[210] The design of social media networks is based on contact chaining and associational linkages between individuals. This information is often enhanced by content-rich data, including facial images, text, video, and audio, frequently with geolocation tagging and time stamps. Certain behavioral biometric signatures may also be derived from these routine digital activities showing patterns in how users post information and use their devices. Experts in the field claim that much of what seems to be anonymous digital presence is relatively easy to de-anonymize by correlating publicly available databases, credit card information, voter records, personal associations, and behavioral patterns—enough information to compile highly individualized dossiers on most general internet users. Such exposure provides a powerful tool for diagramming a network's composition and identifying the individuals operating within them, calling to mind Johann Goethe's maxim, "Tell me with whom you consort and I will tell you who you are."[211]

Legal scholar and retired general Charles Dunlap has suggested that the expanding availability of "big data" and new cyber tools may soon enable "the hyper-personalization of war," leading to the overt targeting of specific individuals both on and off the battlefield. Dunlap notes a "nearly endless number of scenarios where adversaries could hyper-personalize conflict via cyber means."[212] This future mode of warfare may already be taking place, exemplified by the recent penetration of computer systems at the Office of Personnel Management, allegedly by Chinese hackers associated with the People's Liberation Army's Third Department, a group charged with military-focused cyber-intelligence gathering. These hackers focused specifically on the personal data, work and medical histories of thousands of government workers, military and intelligence personnel, and defense contractors, including information on friends, family members, and associates derived from security clearance forms.[213]

One interesting facet that has evolved from the increased availability of open source data and social media content has been the democratization of intelligence. During the Cold War era, the use of advanced technical collection platforms was limited to a handful of major military powers. However, in the age of iWar, small groups, commercial entities, and even individual actors now have the ability to gather information independently and use it for a variety of purposes. Retailers routinely gather detailed information about spending habits, credit histories, websurfing histories, social network postings, and demographic information for market research and precisely targeted advertising.

Similar methods have been used by free-lance intelligence analysts, impressively demonstrated in 2013 when a blogger from England used social media sources to substantiate reports of the Syrian government using chemical-weapons against opposition targets in a Damascus suburb. The same individual later confirmed reports that the Free Syrian Army had obtained anti-aircraft guns, then was able to closely track the tactical progress of Syrian rebels and detail their development of improvised weapons.[214] Another recent example involved "crowd sourced" intelligence derived from a geotagged social media post containing photos of Russian military vehicles moving through Ukraine.[215] This growing database, developed entirely from user-generated reports aggregated on a commercial platform, has become a virtual catalogue of incursions by Russian troops, equipment, and ceasefire violations.

Despite the clear value of such tools, there are significant challenges in using much of the content obtained from social media and user-generated content.

From an analytical perspective, there is the difficult task of filtering potentially useful data from the massive amount of digital clutter, noise, and misinformation. A second issue is one of attribution, specifically knowing the identity of the individual behind the information. As the classic *New Yorker* cartoon prophetically observed in 1993, "On the internet, nobody knows you're a dog." Unlike with biometrics, online digital identities are created, not inherited. These are sometime referred to as "cyber personas" and represent how a user is identified to the larger network through digital attributes such as email address, computer IP address, or cell phone number.[216] However, these identities can be engineered, concealed, and manipulated for specific purposes.

Most savvy social media users practice at least some forms of operational security, while many others intentionally operate behind veils of fictitious identity and deception. Cyberspace is rife with fake twitter accounts, digital avatars, and using anonymizing software that conceals identity. Jihadist forums now advise participants on sophisticated measures for avoiding detection when browsing, including steps for removing geolocation and metadata from cell phone images.[217] Increasingly, OPSEC-savvy militants are also using encrypted messaging apps such as WhatsApp and Kik, or data-destroying apps such as Wickr and Surespot that make it very difficult for legitimate authorities to identify actors and track their communications. The vast amount of deception and misinformation in the cyber domain has spawned a cottage industry of firms specializing in verifying social media accounts using information such as geo-tracking, metadata, speech, and content analysis to identify imposters and fictitious identities.[218]

The challenge for legitimate operators is in linking the cyber persona to the individual behind the digital representation. As one cryptographer and security expert recently noted, "We're living in a world where we can't easily tell the difference between a couple of guys in a basement apartment and the North Korean government," in effect creating "an arms race between attackers and those that want to identify them."[219] In response to such challenges, the CIA reportedly is undertaking a broad restructuring based in part on the realization that this new environment has fundamentally changed how espionage is conducted. As part of this new approach, the organization reportedly will increase cyber capabilities across every category of operations, for example, using cyber tools for "confirming the identities of targets of drone strikes or penetrating Internet-savvy adversaries such as the Islamic State."[220]

All of these issues link back to the foundational components of the iWar paradigm, **individualization**, **identity**, and **information**. As identity-based screening and personalized targeting become normalized, the issue of identity and attribution will only grow as an operational concern. For this reason, it is important also to consider how the concept of identity itself may change in the future.

iWar and the Future of Identity.

The concept of identity can be frustratingly abstract, particularly as compared to more concrete aspects of national security strategy and warfare. Arguably, the very meaning of identity is in the midst of a revolutionary transformation, with changes that undoubtedly will have major implications on how iWar is waged in the future. This section briefly considers some of these factors and offers speculations on the social, economic, and technical trends likely to shape the meaning of identity as it relates to future national security challenges.

As this monograph has posited, identity within the iWar paradigm has become an operational "center of gravity" for networked adversaries, nonstate actors, and individual combatants. As Carl von Clausewitz conceptualized the term, it represents "the hub of all power and movement, on which everything depends."[221] In conventional conflicts, this generally refers to an adversary's military capabilities, those assets and qualities enabling it to apply combat power on the battlefield. In the case of irregular warfare and insurgencies, the center of gravity generally is viewed in terms of political legitimacy, security factors, and the ability to exert influence over a population. At its essence, it represents an adversary's source of strength, as well as its greatest weakness and vulnerability.[222] In the age of iWar, the new center of gravity has become identity.

The cohesiveness of a network comes from identity and the associational relationships among its members. Identity is what distinguishes social networks from bureaucracies. Whereas bureaucracies are depersonalized and operate on the basis of procedure and protocol, social networks derive strength from interpersonal connections, bonds of trust, and expectations that are perceived rather than codified. The integrity of an adversary network depends upon the confidence that identities can be internally trusted and externally protected. Denying anonymity to an adversary's network deprives it of its unique power. As actors are identified, connections are exposed, and activities are attributed, the network becomes vulnerable. With this exposure, it loses the ability to operate, to maneuver, to plan, and to communicate.

As the glue of network cohesion, it is important to understand how the concept of identity is changing. Many of these transformations are due to recent technical innovations that are changing how identity information is created, stored, exchanged, and verified. Additionally, social factors are eroding the state's traditional function as the sole authority for ascribing official identity. Individuals as well as corporations are taking the lead in defining new identity concepts and creating the context for how they are used. Economic forces are also playing a role, such as the personalization of commerce and growth of the "sharing economy." These changes are introducing new mechanisms for identity verification, transactional attribution, and the increasing importance placed on reputational interest. As a result, new forms of digital identity are evolving in order to verify who is participating in these exchanges and whether or not these agents can be trusted.

These trends suggest the beginnings of a new system of identity governance. In this environment, individuals and commercial interests will challenge state authority in the mediation of identity. Governments will likely retain some powers to define the terms of official identity by means of controlling access to certain privileges and benefits; however, individuals will increasingly have the capability to control, negotiate, and manipulate their own identities, particularly within the digital environment. Commercial interests will emerge as for-hire facilitators helping to manage these personal identities, either as an explicit customer service or for the purpose of commoditizing identity information for use by third parties.

These changes reflect a paradox of how identity will evolve in society. On one hand, these technologies are enabling ever-greater personalization of experience. This is seen in the expanding use of social media, the individualization of education and medicine, technologies for continuous bio-monitoring, and mobile apps optimized for individual habits, personal preferences, and daily patterns of life. On the other, countervailing forces are pushing for improved technical options to protect privacy and personal information, and to ensure anonymity in the digital environment. This is reflected in the expanding use of darknets, strong encryption, and crypto-currencies providing individuals with the ability to communicate securely and conduct their transactions free from surveillance.

Public ambivalence over privacy and personal security issues generally reflect this tension. According to a recent Pew survey, some 93 percent of U.S. adults consider it important to be in control of who can get information about them; however, far fewer (63 percent) feel it is important to be able to "go around in public without always being identified."[223] Yet, survey results also suggest that most Americans are somewhat resigned to the fact that much of their digital activity does not remain private and secure, and even fewer feel that they have much power to control how this data is used.[224] Furthermore, even as Americans profess a desire for digital anonymity, very few take proactive technical measures to enhance privacy or protect online activity from surveillance. These conflicting attitudes are likely to remain in tension and will play a significant role in shaping the future of identity, including its relationship to national security. Perhaps most importantly, the rapid pace of technical change likely means that government will be in a reactive rather than proactive role shaping how this future identity concept evolves.

One change that is likely to have major implications for individuals as well as governments is the idea of identity merger. Today, identity information remains somewhat heterogeneous in terms of its format and how it is stored and used. This traditional identity construct is like a two-dimensional mosaic formed from a plurality of nonoverlapping, distinctly formatted bits of information. This is represented through a combination of sources including state-sanctioned identity documents (passports and birth certificates), unofficial biographic information (newspaper articles, yearbooks, and club memberships), bio-informational data (medical records, prescriptions, and insurance documents), and digital media (social networking, email, and phone records). This legacy construct contains an enormous amount of identity information; however, much of this data is highly fragmented and perishable (in physical form and paper records), or maintained in formats making the information difficult to discover, correlate, and analyze. Additionally, these traditional identity markers generally are based on explicit content and declared associations such as family names, phone numbers, physical address, employer, social security numbers, etc.

The characteristics of a new identity construct are likely to be very different from the existing paradigm. It will be less of a mosaic and more of a homogeneous composite that is defined by deeply embedded relationships derived from analytical correlations rather than explicit information. These implicit identities will not be defined by format and will blur the existing distinctions between biographic, biometric, behavioral, and digital information. These composite identities will be persistent, cumulative, and associative — meaning that they will be based on information that endures forever in digital archives, is constantly accumulating as new data points, and contextually enriched through deep correlation to other people, places, and activities. These new identities will not exist as discrete nodes of data, but rather will be defined in the context of their relationship to other things. Thus, this future identity concept will be one that is inherently networked, temporally deep, and multidimensional in ways that current identities are not.

A hint of this future is already apparent in how individuals are using smart phone technologies and other networked devices. Many of these are already enabled with multi-modal biometric authentication (fingerprint, iris, facial, and keystroke/gesture recognition). This means that any activity associated with a particular device can be unambiguously linked to other unique identity signatures such as voice and data transmissions, behavioral patterns, geospatial movements, and social network activity. One implication of this identity merger will be the potential for more powerful means of passive monitoring and surveillance. As digital identities increasingly are merged with other biometric data, behavioral patterns, and contextual biographic information, acts of intentional deception may also become easier to detect. Under Secretary of Defense for Intelligence Mike Vickers recently observed how the tracking of individuals around the globe has become easier in recent years due to "the digital dust that we all leave around as we lead our lives."[225]

Google is already demonstrating some practical examples of this changing identity concept with its Project Abacus, a real-time security system using a combination of facial recognition, voice detection, and behavioral data to enable continuous device authentication without the use of traditional passwords.[226] The next phase of iWar is likely to focus on such nontraditional signatures and sensors able to detect and resolve a wide range of discrete and ambiguous identifiers. This will be combined with new analytical tools able to discover and correlate these attributes from massive data streams of heterogeneous and fragmented information. The final section of this monograph will examine several of these emerging technology areas, discuss the potential application of these tools, and consider how they may shape how iWar is waged in the future.

TECHNOLOGY FUTURES: WAGING IWAR IN THE NEXT GENERATION

The following scenario and technology discussion addresses three interrelated tasks that are central to iWar: **Identity Discovery**, **Operational Attribution**, and **Mapping the Network**. In describing these tasks, this section explores a number of emerging technology areas just beyond the operational horizon. While intended to be realistic, it should be noted that this scenario presupposes certain organizational capabilities, operational methods, and information sharing policies not yet in existence. Nevertheless, the hypothetical case study provides a context for examining how a range of new technical tools could soon be applied for operational use and shape how iWar is waged in the future.

Task One: Identity Discovery.

A disheveled young man speaking in accented English enters Istanbul's Ataturk Airport with a one-way ticket to Amsterdam. His shoes are covered in mud, shirt slightly tattered, and his appearance suggests several days without bathing. As he enters the immigration control area, the man is visibly apprehensive as he approaches the customs agent. He has no checked luggage and only a small carry-on bag containing a cell phone, USB drive, travel documents, and a few personal items. As the agent scans his boarding card, the Passenger Name Record data appears on the screen giving the name, address and a credit card number associated with the ticket purchase. The agent then notices an alert message indicating that the passport number was recently listed in INTERPOL's Stolen and Lost Travel Document database. On closer examination, the agent notices that the passport picture appears somewhat different from the man's appearance. Based on these concerns, the suspect is pulled aside for secondary screening and not permitted to board the flight.

The first challenge of this scenario is resolving the identity of a suspicious individual potentially traveling under false documentation. Several standard biometric modalities are currently in use for establishing identity and screening individuals against watch list information. These include the most commonly used biometric modalities of facial, fingerprint, and iris. While facial recognition remains somewhat less reliable than other biometric modalities for identity verification, it has advantages over other modalities that typically require subject cooperation and direct contact. Of the standard modalities, facial recognition has seen perhaps the most change in recent years due in part to a rapidly expanding range of commercial applications.

Recent performance evaluations of facial recognition algorithms conducted by the National Institute of Standards and Technology reported that overall accuracy in the field has improved up to 30 percent since 2010.[227] For example, improved algorithms have enhanced applications for detecting fraudulent passport and driver license applications, methods for access control and area surveillance, and digital forensics in criminal investigations. Among commercial apps, Facebook has accumulated what experts estimate to be the largest facial recognition database in existence, used for identifying and tagging individuals appearing in user-generated photos.[228] According to the company's research team, its face matching software has achieved over 97 percent accuracy for matching faces between two unfamiliar photos, performance levels roughly equivalent to human capability. This includes photos taken under variable lighting conditions and even in some cases where the subject is not facing directly into the camera.[229]

Conventional facial recognition apps generally work by applying algorithms to extract features from images using one of two approaches. The first is geometric, or feature based, which decomposes the facial structure into components known as eigenfaces. These components are then compared with other images by measuring distance between respective features. A second approach, referred to as photometric, or view based, uses a statistical approach for distilling an image into values and comparing them with known templates.[230] With either method, the major technical challenges include dealing with low-quality images, changes in subject appearance, and pose variations.[231] Additionally, there are a number of technical limitations in terms of capturing usable imagery at long distances, during nighttime, and from low-resolution images of the kind obtained from webcams, ATM cameras, or surveillance video.[232]

Facial identification based on a combination of 3D data and infrared images has been demonstrated as one potential method for enhancing current approaches.[233] This can be accomplished by converting 2D images to 3D avatars, using mathematical modeling in order to capture data lost in standard images. Additionally, 3D image scanning combined with thermal modeling offers a means of potentially overcoming challenges with pose variation and lighting conditions that can reduce accuracy. These methods are also technically more difficult to spoof than standard approaches.

Current 3D scanning technologies are better suited to access control rather than surveillance; however, other developments may soon offer expanded utility. Some of these include the use of face-texture analysis, improved algorithms for image extraction from infrared video, as well as methods for using composite images derived from multiple video frames.[234] Other approaches involve the use of 3D topology and cameras that are able to capture data outside the visible spectrum such as near-infrared and long-wave infrared thermal. Such methods might also be used to collect physiological signatures, including temperature, pulse, and blood pressure.[235]

Beyond imaging technologies, the next major gains in facial recognition are likely to come from a combination of increased processing power and improvements in the use of artificial intelligence (AI). AI refers generally to the subfield of computer science dealing with algorithms focused on tasks traditionally requiring human analysis such as visual perception, speech recognition, and abstract problem solving. AI is often associated with the concept of "big data" due to the fact that these large datasets generally must be analyzed through computational methods. AI algorithms are generally very useful for analyzing and interpreting this data to reveal patterns, trends, and embedded associations.[236] Within the field of AI, a distinct area called machine learning involves the use of specialized algorithms able to "learn" from the data itself and offer predictive models by analyzing patterns. One class of machine learning known as "deep learning" uses mathematical formulas to replicate "neural networks" by simulating the analytical processes of the human brain. These methods have demonstrated significant potential for improving the accuracy and power of existing biometric modalities, particularly in the areas of facial, speaker, and voice recognition.

The concept for neural networks has existed for several decades; however, practical applications were limited by computing power and the lack of sufficiently large datasets to optimize "training." This training occurs by process repetition that "teaches" the computer how to recognize increasingly more complex features contained within the data, such as from collections of images or sound files. For example, one of the more famous technical challenges in the field of image recognition involves the relatively simple human task of teaching a computer to identify images of cats among a collection of unrelated photos. Recently Google researchers demonstrated a significant improvement at this task, using deep learning methods to sort through and identify target images from some 10 million examples contained in YouTube videos.[237] Similar methods have been used to increase the speed and accuracy of commercial image recognition applications such as those used by Facebook, Google, Microsoft, and Twitter.[238]

The application of deep learning methods and neural networks are likely to offer significant performance improvements for image and video analytics, potentially enabling rapid searches and matching from enormous repositories of media files. This task represents one of the major technical hurdles in the era of "big data." For example, the FBI's biometric database is expected to contain some 52 million facial images by 2015, while the Department of State already has an even larger holding of photos from visa applicants.[239] Sorting through these repositories presents a relatively well-defined task of matching within a closed system containing uniform data and strict controls on image quality. However, a much greater technical challenge is involved in exploiting information from unstructured databases such as sifting through massive amounts of social media content in search of meaningful correlations. This is especially true for collections containing ambiguous, unformatted content or files with associated metadata. Other challenges involve matching heterogeneous data such as the task of comparing images obtained from visible light versus near-infrared systems.

Several recent prototypes have demonstrated how neural networks might help to overcome some of these limitations such as the ability to identify facial images captured at an angle or when partially occluded. Researchers have applied these methods to improve automated detection algorithms for video files, moving the technology a step closer to having the capability of real-time analysis of digitized video or closed-circuit television (CCTV) footage.[240] The future gold standard for facial recognition will be the capability for noncontact collection, at a reasonable range, among multiple individuals, with near real-time identification. Some currently available technologies hint at the direction this capability may move. For example, one new commercial product is able to capture facial images from live video feeds, then instantly compile any identity-related content from social media sites and other open sources to create a real-time subject profile.

There have also been recent improvements in existing technologies for enhancing the speed and flexibility of biometric enrollment, such as collecting iris images in just a few seconds and the capability for noncontact fingerprint capture. High-resolution cameras are now producing recognition-quality images from a distance of several meters under certain conditions, with some prototypes even extending this effect range out to 100-200 meters.[241] One potential use of this capability was recently demonstrated by a group claiming to have obtained a useable fingerprint biometric from the German Defense Minister derived only from a digital photograph, taken at a distance, during a public speaking engagement. The image reportedly was obtained using a commercially available digital camera and a common fingerprint scanning algorithm.[242] Various methods are also in development for noncontact fingerprint recognition on mobile and other digital devices. Similar progress is being made in capturing useable iris data under bright sunlight conditions—a major limiting factor of this modality.[243] Another company has demonstrated an iris scanning prototype able to collect usable images at more than 30 yards against a stationary subject; however, such technologies remain years away from operational use.[244] Other efforts are exploring variations on the basic modalities such as using the blood vessel patterns in the eye which, unlike iris and retinal scans, can be captured with standard digital cameras rather than infrared light emitters.

Among the standard modalities, another important goal involves improved methods for multi-modal data integration, specifically bringing together iris, fingerprint, and facial imaging into a composite "pattern of life" profile of individual subjects.[245] Beyond these technologies, a number of nontradition biometric modalities are gradually moving toward operational use, including vascular pattern, ear structure, hand geometry, gait, odor, palm print, and electrocardiograph. Another nontraditional modality now being used on a wider scale is the identification of scars, marks, and tattoos. The FBI's next generation identification database recently integrated this capability, offering both image matching and queries based on descriptive key words.[246] While not uniquely identifying in isolation, such tools offer another means for multi-modal verification that potentially improves accuracy when linked with other attributes such as DNA profiles, biographic data, behavioral patterns, and digital and media signatures.

Another modality with recent gains in performance has been the field speaker recognition. As a biometric, automated speaker recognition systems can "extract, characterize, and recognize the information in the speech signal conveying speaker identity."[247] Generally this can be done with just a brief voice sample providing enough data to measure an individual's unique vocal traits and produce a biometric quality "voiceprint." Many current efforts in the field have been focused on identity authentication and fraud detection for use in banking services, call center operations, and for digital device interface. This has led to a rapid expansion in the number of individuals using this technology with one industry research study estimating that, by 2019, some five billion people will have created a personal voiceprint.[248] Experts speculate that some 65 million unique voiceprints may already be contained in U.S. law enforcement and intelligence community databases — a number certain to expand exponentially in coming years.[249]

As a biometric, voice offers several distinct advantages over other modalities. It has been called an "invisible" biometric since it does not require direct contact for collection as voiceprints can be obtained from a range of sensors (microphone, telephones, computers, etc.). However, there are several limitations of current technology, including difficulty in cross-channel comparisons between landline, cellular, or microphone recordings, as well as issues dealing with ambient noise, language variations, or unusual phonation such as whispering. Another major technical challenge entails dealing with overlapping speech from multiple speakers on a single audio sample.[250]

Once voice data is collected, the traditional approaches of speaker recognition generally apply statistical models to represent variations in sound forms, or phonemes, unique to an individual's voice.[251] Hidden Markov Models (HMM) have been the dominant statistical technique for text-dependent speaker recognition (when there is prior knowledge of the text to be spoken). A related method, known as Gaussian Mixture Models, is often used for text-independent, or extemporaneous speech, not requiring cooperation by the speaker. In both cases, digitized voice patterns are compared to stored voiceprints in order to produce a recognition decision. Similar statistical models are applied to other pattern recognition tasks such as natural language processing, handwriting, and gesture analysis. The HMM method is behind the Army's current VIBES prototype used for identifying and tracking individuals and analyzing tactical communications networks.[252]

As with facial recognition technology, recent advances in machine learning and increased processing power have led to significant performance improvements. Neural networks are now being used on large databases of sound files for identification of progressively more complex combinations of phonemes. This enables the programs to "learn" over time, without human intervention and better deal with ambiguity in syntax as well as variations in usage and dialect. Deep learning methods and neural networks may also provide approaches for enhancing low-quality signal data by filtering out unwanted sounds, removing noisiness, and even disambiguating multiple voices on a single channel.[253] This could also overcome some of the technical difficulties encountered with audio type mismatch. The Defense Advanced Research Projects Agency (DARPA) is exploring solutions to some of these issues through its Robust Automatic Transcription of Speech program aimed at separating speech from background noise as well as related tasks such as determining the languages being spoken from an audio file and isolating key words within that sample.[254]

Researchers are also experimenting with novel applications derived from voiceprint data such as determining an individual's emotional state. One such example involves biomedical screening of neurological disorders using a combination of markers derived from motor control functions linked to speech and facial expression. A team from the Massachusetts Institute of Technology's (MIT) Lincoln Laboratory recently demonstrated an application using facial and vocal biomarkers as a predictive tool for analyzing an individual's cognitive state.[255] The Department of

Homeland Security is exploring related capabilities for use in checkpoint screening, for example, using a combination of facial movements, voice samples, and physiological sensors for detecting respiratory, cardio, thermal, and iris reaction as a means of identifying hostile intent or suspicious behavior among crowds.[256]

Some researchers speculate that these methods may soon enable computers to surpass humans in the ability to perceive basic emotions. DARPA has demonstrated the utility of automated tools for identifying psychological distress, depression, and anxiety.[257] There have also been successful examples of applying facial recognition software to code emotional expressions based on distinct movements of facial muscles, eyes, cheeks, lips, and other features. A recent commercial prototype achieved an accuracy rate on the order of 97 percent in the identification of six basic emotions, and 77 percent for some compound emotions.[258]

Beyond the standard modalities, the growing field of behavioral biometrics potentially offers a range of new methods for establishing identity by indirect means. In general terms, behavioral biometrics refers to characteristics that are learned or acquired over time rather than those based primarily on biology. For instance, these include skills, style, preference, knowledge, and motor skills that people use to accomplish everyday tasks.[259] Some common examples in current use involve handwriting, keystroke, mouse dynamics, or walking gait analysis. Other examples include the identification of distinguishing behavioral patterns derived from activities such as email routines, device interactions, and credit card usage.

Behavioral biometrics has a number of advantages over traditional biometrics, most notably the potential for remote or noncompliant collection. Although behavioral biometrics are often less accurate than biologic measures, they can be used in conjunction with other modalities or applied indirectly for identifying characteristics of individuals within a larger population. For instance, this might include identifying a group of individuals with a distinguishing attribute such as word knowledge, mathematical aptitude, or skill at a specific task such as speaking a foreign language or flying an airplane. While not uniquely identifying in isolation, such contextual information could be useful in analyzing networks by categorizing the functions of individual members or network nodes.

Other activity patterns such as email usage or web surfing offer the possibility of deriving unique user identification with the advantage of nonobtrusive collection. Multiple studies have demonstrated how unique behavioral profiles can be derived from the peculiarities of email usage, including message stylization, temporal activity, structure, and other variables.[260] This has obvious applications for resolving ambiguous identities derived from user accounts shared by multiple individuals or accessing public computers. Similar applications have been developed to spot aberrant behavior on social media platforms and detecting fake Twitter and Facebook accounts. Analysis of behavioral patterns can help confirm the authenticity of anonymous actors on social media or detect pattern similarities between multiple users across platforms. Behavioral biometrics can also be applied to help identify online deception campaigns by analyzing linguistic cues, usage patterns, social connections, and physical locations to classify the identities behind the posts. For example, similar methods were recently used to analyze postings from Russian military personnel suspected of mobilizing for operations in Ukraine.[261]

Another example of a common behavioral biometric is the use of credit card patterns for fraud protection by the banking industry. This technique applies statistical methods to identify aberrant behaviors such as unusual transactions, new geographical locations, or simultaneous card use at multiple locations. One vendor in the field has refined a method for analyzing more than 400 bio-behavioral, cognitive, and physiological traits to create highly individualized user profiles.[262] These techniques have become commonplace in bank security and other applications where anonymous metadata can be used to analyze an individual's unique behavioral attributes. A team from MIT's Media Lab demonstrated this capability when they identified some 90 percent of individuals from a sample group based only on the dates and locations of a handful of credit card transactions combined with social media metadata. This was accomplished without prior knowledge of names, addresses, or other information relating to the cardholder.[263]

Behavioral biometrics are also modernizing approaches to traditional modalities such as writing analysis, a technique used for many years as an identifying tool in document forensics. However, in the digital age, there are fewer written documents available for analysis; therefore, methods have evolved for analysis of "digital handwriting" or dynamic signatures based on the unique way a user types, holds, and manipulates a digital device. These techniques are now being applied for identity authentication with mobile devices using cognitive-biometric attributes based on factors such as handedness, hand tremor, eye-hand coordination, keystroke analysis, and other identifiable patterns embedded within human-machine interactions.[264] Research has found these behavioral patterns to be "complex, nuanced, and instinctive," therefore a highly accurate method of identifying individuals.[265] Some recent commercial examples of advanced dynamic signature authentication can track unique identity attributes across four dimensions, including pressure, swiftness, and shape of finger strokes against a touch screen, as well as the speed and acceleration of gestures.[266]

Specialists in the field have also applied deep learning techniques for analysis of gesture and motion control to enable unique activity recognition. Some research suggests that these motion patterns are just as identifying as fingerprints. For example, one recent experiment used unique "egocentric video biometrics" derived from raw video footage taken from head and body-mounted cameras. In this case, the unique biometric markers were obtained from as little as four seconds of footage by tracking "optical flow" through each frame of the video.[267] One potential application would be an ability to locate all videos shot by a single user from within a large database of digital files, even without descriptive metadata. Another recent demonstration applied deep learning methods to improve the performance of built-in sensors on mobile devices (accelerometers, cameras, and microphones) in order to classify whether a user was performing certain kinds of activities.[268] Similar techniques have been developed for biometric authentication from computer mouse manipulation and fitness tracking devices. Most of these behavioral biometric applications are now being used for improving device security; however, they potentially provide a means of remote identification. This could be invaluable information when combined with precise geolocation from a mobile device or correlation with other social media activity. As humans increasingly maintain near-continual interaction with their digital devices, the field of behavioral biometrics will offer techniques well-suited for deriving identity information from these activities.

Another field of emerging biometric modalities is the area of "soft biometrics." These are characteristics with identifying qualities but lacking distinctiveness and permanence to differentiate positively between any two individuals.[269] Examples include traits such as gender, hair color, height, weight, body proportions, eye color, or ethnicity. Another category of soft biometrics includes activity-based characteristics such as uniquely acquired skills or specialized knowledge. Although less identifying than standard modalities, soft biometrics can offer some advantages over biologic and behavioral attributes as a tool for screening and analysis. First, much of the data can be obtained nonobtrusively or derived from low-quality video footage, thus making it useful for high-throughput surveillance applications. Second, unlike technical signatures, soft biometrics can be expressed more easily in natural language, thus making for easier categorization based on verbal descriptions of physical characteristics.[270] This issue relates to the so-called "semantic gap" or the difference between how humans verbally express distinct physical attributes versus how they are represented as biometric signatures.

The central problem of the "semantic gap" is that physical descriptions from eyewitness reports are not easily translatable into machine language for computer assisted search and analysis. Some new approaches in this area involve improved translation of semantic descriptions into usable categorizations for an automated search of images and surveillance video.[271] This kind of semantic labeling potentially provides a powerful enhancement for computer-assisted screening. This may lead to improved algorithms for matching eyewitness sketches with digital face images. Other researchers have demonstrated how generic attribute descriptions such as clothing types, hair color, and gender can be used as criteria for an automated search through large volumes of surveillance video data in order to find persons matching a particular subject profile.[272] While these methods are currently limited by factors such as video quality and crowd density, with improvement they may offer another useful tool in combination with other biometric modalities and contextual information. See the following scenario.

> Based on the INTERPOL alert, the suspect was held for additional questioning. After refusing to discuss his identity or explain the discrepancies from the passport photo, the Directorate General of the Turkish National Police sent his basic biometric data (iris, fingerprint, and facial scan) through the local INTERPOL liaison office for analysis. Within the hour, the INTERPOL HQ notified the Turkish authorities that the passport had been reported stolen some 6 months prior. INTERPOL also reported that the suspect had been declared a person of interest by the U.S. Government based on a match from the FBI's biometric repository. Based on this information, the U.S. legal attaché at the American Embassy in Ankara requested that Turkish authorities keep the man in custody pending further investigation. At the request of the U.S. ambassador, a regionally based Identity Resolution team was deployed to Istanbul to assist Turkish authorities in the ongoing investigation.

OPERATIONAL ATTRIBUTION

The next section discusses emerging technologies that could be applied to the task of operational attribution, or the linking of an identity to specific locations, incidents, and activities. These include a variety of biometric, forensic, and analytical tools that could be leveraged to assist in developing a subject's operational profile. See the following scenario.

> Twenty-four hours later, the Identity Resolution team arrived in Istanbul and began work in collaboration with local authorities. During the preceding day, a check of U.S. Government databases resulted in a confirmed match from the DoD's Biometric Enabled Watchlist. The information revealed that the suspect had been held at the U.S. detention facility at Camp Bucca, Iraq, in 2008 following a Special Operations raid against a suspected IED production facility. The man was released to Iraqi authorities some 17 months later. The report further identified the man as a British national of Jordanian descent. Additional information provided by Dutch authorities through INTERPOL indicated that the man had resided temporarily in Amsterdam a year earlier; however, he departed that country and was suspected of participating as a foreign fighter in Syria. Based on this initial information, the Turkish authorities provided the Identity Resolution team with access to the man's cell phone and personal items. During a subject interview the team collected a voiceprint for analysis and received permission to take soil samples and trace materials from his clothing, as well as a buccal swab for DNA analysis. Turkish authorities also provided CCTV video of the man's arrival and movements through the airport.

Over the last decade, there have been major advances in the use of DNA analysis for military and security functions. As a tool for identity verification it offers the advantages of being unique and unalterable. Like fingerprints, DNA is a latent identifier, meaning it can be obtained forensically without direct physical contact with a subject. It also offers a higher matching confidence than any other biometric and forensic method. For example, there is approximately an 86 percent chance of correctly matching a latent fingerprint against a record in the FBI's biometric database. Conversely, DNA forensics provides near perfect statistical assurance of matching when samples are properly collected and processed.[273]

Currently, the most common technique used for forensic DNA analysis is the short tandem repeat (STR) process that evaluates specific STR regions found in nuclear DNA.[274] The STR profile provides the individual's unique genotype based on regions of the chromosome, called loci, having a high degree of variability between individuals. STR analysis is typically used for body fluids, skin cells, bones, and hairs, and offers an extremely accurate method for identifying a particular individual as the source of an evidence sample.[275] STR analysis has advantages over other methods in terms of sensitivity, shorter processing time, and a higher level of statistical discrimination. Once a sample is processed, this data can be translated into a CODIS-compatible message format then uploaded into a DNA database.[276] Y-STR analysis is a similar method used exclusively on the male Y-chromosome. This technique is often applied for genealogical and paternity testing, sexual assaults, missing persons, and some intelligence applications; however, due to the fact that multiple relatives share the same Y-DNA, it is not yet possible to derive unique identifications from this analysis. The expeditionary forensic labs deployed in Iraq and Afghanistan generally used a combination of these methods of nuclear DNA analysis.

Traditionally, the sequencing process has been the major bottleneck of DNA forensics; however, process improvements, miniaturization, and automation have greatly reduced many of these hurdles. Recent advances in mircofluidics, the handling of very small volumes of fluids, has revolutionized DNA analysis and enabled high-throughput sequencing. These new "rapid DNA" methods generally describe a fully automated (hands-free) process for developing CODIS core STR profiles from reference samples. Various commercial providers offer fully integrated systems capable of performing STR analysis in less than 2 hours. Rapid DNA instruments are not yet approved for domestic crime scene forensics; however, the FBI Laboratory and federal agencies, including the U.S. Army Crime Laboratory, are conducting test and evaluation for future accreditation and operational use.[277]

Another limitation of current technologies is the need for trained technicians working in controlled laboratory environments; however, recent prototypes are overcoming many of these challenges. One recent example is the accelerated nuclear DNA equipment (ANDE) system, a device about the size of a desktop printer and able to process as many as five DNA samples in 90 minutes. Importantly, this system can be operated by nontechnical personnel, outside of a laboratory setting, and reliably produce forensic-quality STR profiles that are fully compatible with CODIS message format.[278] U.S. Special Operations forces have already used similar devices in forward locations and, within the next 5 years, hope to field-test a miniaturized, battery-powered version of DNA readers, allowing forces to collect DNA in a tactical environment and instantly compare results to a remote database.[279]

In the next major advancement, next generation sequencing (NextGen DNA sequencing) methods will soon offer powerful new capabilities using single-nucleotide polymorphisms (SNP) analysis based on variations at a single site in the DNA. These sites are scattered throughout the human genome and play a large role in determining an individual's susceptibility to disease and response to vaccines and other environmental agents. NextGen DNA sequencing methods use exome sequencing (a subset of all DNA across all chromosomes) to analyze thousands more SNPs at a time and produce a higher level of discrimination than current STR analysis, even from degraded samples.[280] These techniques can help to overcome one of the significant limitations of current STR analysis, specifically the challenge of dealing with DNA mixtures involving genetic materials from multiple individuals. This is a significant concern in scenarios such as IED factories or crime scenes where more than one person has handled physical evidence. NextGen DNA sequencing will offer more robust capabilities for characterization of these identities as well as decreasing the cost and speed of analysis.[281]

The SNP profiles derived from NextGen DNA sequencing methods have also demonstrated significant potential for analyzing variations between individual genomes, opening a door to novel applications beyond basic identification matching. These may include deriving bio-geographic ancestry, extended kinship mapping, and surname prediction from genetic samples.[282] Such methods could be particularly useful in geographic regions where there are dense familial and tribal relationships that are closely related to targeted networks. These methods have already been used for deriving familial relationships from unknown DNA samples as part of criminal investigations.[283]

Even with the increased analytical power of current methods, SNP genotyping still uses less than 0.1 percent of human genetic material. However, advances in high-throughput sequencing will soon offer the potential for whole genome analysis, leading to improved prediction of visible physical characteristics, also known as forensic DNA phenotyping.[284] Full genome analysis has already demonstrated reasonable accuracy in predicting features such as eye and hair color. Some experts suggest it may soon predict skin color, freckling, baldness, hair curliness, tooth shape, and even age. One research team recently demonstrated a three-dimensional modeling program able to depict a "genetic face" based on sex and ancestry mix determined from the DNA. The image can then be refined based on 24 genetic variants from 20 genes known to be involved in facial variation.[285] While intriguing, such applications are still new, controversial, and not yet permissible in most legal proceedings.

The complexity and expense of whole genome sequencing has dropped dramatically in recent years, from millions of dollars a decade ago to a few thousand at present. In addition to a wide range of medical applications, this capability could also offer improved techniques for epigenetic analysis, or interpretation of gene expressions caused by specific environmental exposure to chemicals, radiation, or other agents. This could lead to more detailed subject trait profiles based on nothing more than residual DNA. Another potentially useful application emerging from whole genome sequencing will be powerful capabilities for metagenomic analysis of materials obtained from environmental samples. This could offer unique characterization of microbial ecologies, for instance, analyzing the recent movements of a subject based on evidence from trace soil, microbial organisms, or pollen samples. This might also be used to detect recent exposure to chemicals or precursor materials of interest.[286] See the following scenario.

As the investigation continued, the Identity Resolution team obtained initial results from the DNA analysis. The suspect's profile matched an unidentified sample catalogued in late-2009 from forensic evidence found at an IED factory in Iraq. Several days later, the team received results from geo-forensic analysis of trace samples obtained from the suspect's clothing. This determined that the dried soil on the man's shoes and pollen in his clothing were consistent with soil texture and vegetation types common in northern Syria, suggesting recent travel from that region. This suspicion was corroborated by exploitation of the cell phone's metadata that provided time and locations of the suspect's most recent travel. The cell phone also contained personal identifying information for a number of associates, including names, addresses, telephone numbers, e-mail addresses, chat user names, and recent text message exchanges with individuals suspected of having links to a known foreign fighter facilitation network. The browser cache also contained a record of several recently accessed social media sites. A number of short videos were extracted from the phone's on-board memory to be analyzed and compared against other media samples posted to online forums frequented by the foreign fighter community. Additionally, the phone's internal sensor data was used to create a biometric profile from stored gesture patterns and keystroke history. Based on the developing body of evidence, the U.S. legal attaché requested that Turkish authorities continue to hold the suspect as the investigation continued.

MAPPING THE NETWORK

Once operational history is established, the next step involves linking identity to other activities, locations, and a wider network of relevant actors. One of the major analytical challenges in this task is uncovering the implicit network connections contained within enormous amounts of unstructured data. As Director of National Intelligence James Clapper recently explained, in the era of big data, the challenge is finding the needles without having to deal with the haystacks.[287] The next section explores some recent advances in areas such as video analytics, natural language processing, and data management, specifically exploring how these technologies are improving methods for sorting, correlating, and analyzing information from a variety of sources. See the following scenario.

As the investigation continued, DNA kinship analysis compared with the CODIS database suggested a possible familial link between the suspect detained in Turkey and another man recently arrested during an FBI raid against a suspected terror cell in Atlanta, Georgia. The cell was accused of conducting pre-operational planning for a possible attack against a U.S. Federal building. Materials seized during the raid included a laptop with pdf. files containing handwritten notes and bomb making instructions. Handwriting and content analysis from the document files suggested a likely match to several documents found in the files of the suspect in Turkey. The laptop seized during the Atlanta raid also contained several video clips taken at an unidentified terrorist training camp. Gesture control analysis from the clips matched those of the video segments obtained from the suspect's cell phone, suggesting that a single individual using that phone camera had recorded all of the training camp videos. Content analysis of the video, including activities, landscape, and individuals, also matched similar videos posted on several social media sites frequented by extremist groups. From this data and other supporting information, the location of the camp was narrowed to a few likely sites. These materials also provided evidence of a direct operational linkage between the suspect in Turkish custody and the planning cell in Atlanta.

The last few years have seen significant advances in video analytics, particularly the use of artificial intelligence for improved content analysis. This field of "computer vision" focuses on these automated methods for processing, interpreting, and analyzing image content. Most conventional methods for sorting and correlating bulk video data still rely on metadata information such as titles and text comments associated with the media rather than the actual content. This presents a major challenge for conducting large-scale multimedia data retrieval, queries, and analysis based only on metadata keywords. Another approach has been to use model-based semantic analysis for identifying content relating to a predefined set of activities. As with other tasks involving complex probabilistic modeling, HMM and related methods has been one approach for pattern recognition of video content.[288]

Artificial intelligence and deep learning methods have potential for improving content-based analysis and aiding discovery of contextual relationships between video data, other media, and information. One recent demonstration involved training a computer to distinguish between a group of men playing Frisbee and a herd of elephants walking in the grass.[289] While seemingly a basic task for humans, this represented a major technical achievement for computers. The evolution of such tools will be critical for rapidly cataloging and analyzing the millions of digital images and video files generated and uploaded onto the Internet each day—an amount that already greatly exceeds what can be done by human analysis. One example highlighting the great potential in this area was recently demonstrated in a commercial application using deep learning software to analyze videos rapidly and recognize some 10,000 different objects and types of scenes within the collection of clips.[290] The software was even able to derive and identify abstract descriptive concepts such as "fun."

A related analytical challenge concerns training computers to interpret and extract highly nuanced content features such as defined social roles. For example, one recent prototype demonstrated the ability to identify the most important individual among a group of people appearing together in a photo.[291] This sort of task depends on deriving complex semantic meaning from subtle visual cues, then translating these visual indicators into useful text descriptions that can be understood by humans or used in computational analysis. Researchers at Google recently demonstrated such a method of translating complicated images into short descriptive sentences. The approach involved training neural networks on two separate but related tasks: first, processing images into mathematical representations based on content, then, second, translating that information into a human-readable text. In this case, the neural network was "trained" from tens of thousands of images that were already tagged with descriptions written by humans.[292]

There is related work in this field on improved methods for document authentication and determining image provenance, a particularly useful tool, given recent examples of image manipulation being used as part of information campaigns. For example, during the 2014 offensive by the Islamic State into Iraq, militants posted pictures of captured helicopters and tanks allegedly taken from Iraqi security forces; however, analysis later revealed that many of the images posted on social media sites turned out to be older file photos. Iran, Russia, and others have also used manipulated images for the purpose of disinformation and deception. One effort focused on overcoming such challenges is the Intelligence Advanced Research Projects Activity "Finder" program designed to help analysts locate non-geotagged imagery from collections of photographs or video clips. This could leverage online crowd-sourcing tools or use image matching techniques based on large reference databases of overhead and ground-based images, including features such as elevation data, surface geology, ground vegetation, local geography, and embedded cultural information. Prototype testing has demonstrated some initial success using data-rich video and imagery files containing relatively recognizable features. However, even in the case of remote locations with less embedded data, the tools were still able to significantly narrow down the search region in some cases.[293]

As with image and video data, the exponential growth of text-based document and media files presents similar technical challenges for analysts. This is the general focus of Natural Language Processing (NLP) technologies, a field of computer science dealing with the task of enabling computers to derive meaning from human language inputs. NLP touches on many of the functional areas already discussed, including tasks such as speech recognition, machine translation, and automated document classification.

As with image analysis, the ability to derive contextual meaning from large amounts of unformatted data and bulk media files is critical for entity discovery and mapping network relationships.

Traditional NLP approaches have applied machine learning approaches and statistical models to make probabilistic determinations based on comparisons to a corpus of sample texts available in digital databases and online collections. This is essentially how Google's voice and translation applications work, by making comparisons to previously translated documents found around the web then determining most likely matches.[294] Once natural language inputs are converted into homogenous data sets, this enables easier discovery of identity attributes and relationship extraction.

As in other areas, advances in artificial intelligence show great promise for improving the accuracy of NLP methods, particularly in the areas of information retrieval and data correlation. Importantly, many of these techniques go far beyond basic machine translation and optical character recognition. These methods may soon enable computers to derive deeper semantic meaning and higher-level functions such as sentiment analysis of social media and advanced data visualization based on embedded linkages between people, places, and activities contained within large amounts of unstructured data.

Some current applications are already appearing in the commercial sector, for instance, using NLP methods for interpreting social media inputs and logically recommending appropriate hashtags and improved methods for understanding a user's implicit intentions behind a series of words entered into a search engine.[295] One artificial intelligence company has applied NLP technologies to enable real-time analysis of multiple communications channels, including news sites, blogs, online forums, and social media to help identify emerging trends and unique behavioral patterns.[296] Importantly, these systems are moving toward an ability to derive contextual meaning without requiring a human analyst in the loop. Both the Defense and Intelligence Advanced Research Projects Agencies have multiple programs in this area and are attempting to apply these technologies for defense and intelligence use. See the following scenario.

> Over the next several weeks, the investigation continued with an analysis of the suspect's digital presence through social media activity, browsing history, and contacts obtained from the phone's data cache. This analysis revealed several useful linkages between various on-line profiles, tweets, geotagged posts, images, and video content linked to a blog. The correlation of these digital signatures provided a basic pattern of life based on recent activities, locations, interactions, and communications through various social media channels. As the team reconstructed the suspect's digital identity map, the investigators were able to infer latent social networks based on correlation with other users sharing similar patterns, habits, locations, and semantic content. This evidence suggested links to several key nodes of a foreign fighter facilitation network and the location of a previously unknown processing facility for newly arriving recruits. Further analysis of propaganda videos posted to several social media sites produced additional high-probability matches with the suspect's facial image, gait, and voiceprint. Separately, the results of a full genome DNA analysis suggested a possibility of the suspect's recent exposure to precursor chemicals commonly used as accelerants for bomb making.

The final section examines how analytical tools for social media and other "big data" sources may offer new capabilities for linking identity signatures to larger network structures, possibly even enabling improved methods for predictive analysis. Social media analysis offers another means of identity discovery and attribute linage across wider networks. Many approaches in this area are based on the study of graph analytics, an interdisciplinary field concerned with information extraction, data management, and visualization.[297] These tasks involve the use of statistical methods for detecting implicit network structures, actor attributes, and embedded relationships.

Some of the complicating factors in this analysis include dealing with the inherent subjectivity of textual data, ambiguous identities, and uncertainty in classifying the relationships between these entities.[298] Many of these cutting edge tools for social media analysis are found in the commercial sector and are currently being used for purposes such as marketing and political forecasting. However, many of these tools clearly have dual-use applications for national security, disaster relief, and law enforcement functions. For example, applications able to geolocate Tweeter feeds and Facebook posts have been used to analyze behavioral patterns and identity attributes from anonymous social media actors.

Others researchers in the field of social media analysis have been able to construct generic identity profiles based on implicit attribute information embedded within the content and structure of network communications such as linguistic patterns, social connections, and expressed preferences. For example, researchers have demonstrated that identity attributes such as age, gender, occupation, education, and even personality traits, can be accurately predicted from the analysis of web browsing activity. Other studies have shown how social media patterns can accurately reveal characteristics such as sexual orientation, ethnicity, and religious and political views.[299] While not explicitly identifying, such data points could provide a strong basis for basic identity profiling and screening.[300] Related work has exploited social media content to generate relatively reliable personality recognition predictions for traits such as extraversion, neuroticism, agreeableness, conscientiousness, and openness.[301]

Much of this work is based on new insights about how the structure of an individual's social network creates a "digital footprint" that, in some instances, can predict latent personality traits and behavioral propensities such as job success, drug use, infidelity, and general level of emotional happiness.[302] Researchers have also applied statistical-relational analysis for improved attribute prediction and classification based on how specific variables are transmitted between individuals based on their social and organizational ties.[303] For instance, this kind of analysis has been used for identifying behavioral propensities of individual actors within larger social communities and used for tasks such as risk-based predictive screening. For example, one UK government screening program for terrorism prevention has developed a model of behavioral indicators as part of its vulnerability assessment framework, applying 22 variables associated with factors such as engagement, intent, and capability. Together these indicators can suggest an individual's vulnerability for being drawn toward violent extremism.[304]

Much of the information required for such analysis may be gleaned from publically available social media data and other open sources. Recently, a team from the King's College International Centre for the Study of Radicalization and Political Violence (ICSR) used social media information and other open data to build profiles of some 700 Western foreign fighters who had traveled to Syria as combatants, compiling as many as 72 data points for each individual. This dataset provided useful insights into identities and operational profiles of individuals joining the movement, as well as significant details about the methods and pathways of their recruitment.[305] Of particular note, this evidence established how the foreign fighter cohorts evolved from clearly identifiable social clusters and groups of friends typically drawn from the same geographic areas.[306]

This example highlights one of the classic applications of social network theory, specifically the dynamics of social influence. Recent work in the field has demonstrated how these techniques can even identify leadership actors and functional roles among members of a network based only on general patterns of activity, communications, and individual attributes.[307] Related areas of research have also demonstrated how social network analysis can be used for deception detection, authorship attribution, sentiment analysis, and opinion mining. This is similar to the idea behind "crowd-sensing" or using aggregate data derived from mobile devices to model general behavioral patterns as well as predicting more specific variables of interest.[308] These methods may also offer new approaches for dynamic social network analysis, a subfield that examines changes in the behavior of social networks over time, an important tool for detecting anomalous behavior within networks and among the individual actors operating within them.[309]

The ongoing conflict in Syria has provided a rich dataset for experimentation. Since the start of hostilities foreign fighters have generated millions of social media posts and enormous amounts of digital content. By some accounts, the Islamic State is linked to some 90,000 message posts each day, involving as many as 30,000 active followers around the globe.[310] One team of researchers recently used this data to develop a detailed network representation of the intercommunal dynamics involved in the conflict. This analysis revealed a surprising level of internal complexity among the factions, including implicit divisions among the protagonists that were not obvious from anecdotal reporting. Importantly, this analysis identified distinct cohorts of social media followers observing the conflict from outside Syria and provided insights into the dynamics of the external media campaign.[311]

Nearly all of these analytical techniques are based on the use of "big data" for identity discovery and attribute correlation. This common, and often misused, term refers not only to the size of the data sets involved but also to the computational tools and statistical methods used to derive meaning from the data. Dealing with the variety and volume of information contained in these massive datasets has created a situation that is "overwhelming and incomprehensible to humans" and requires improved methodologies for turning this data into coherent information.[312] Some of these techniques have already been described at length; however, a few examples illustrate how these large datasets might be used in the future for improving identity discovery, operational attribution, and network mapping.

One recent example of a "big data" tool is the DARPA-sponsored Memex search engine. This application builds infographics based on relationships between web pages, specifically those residing in so-called "dark web" networks like Tor where IP addresses are obscured.[313] Unlike standard search engines designed to sift through text and images, Memex uses embedded information such as geo-coordinates encoded into photos, handwritten numbers within images, and even background scenes from photos that can be compared independently from the other objects in the picture. From this information Memex produces a networked schematic based on the implicit relationships embedded within the nonindexed data, including things like phone numbers, street addresses, and individual names.

Another example of a big data-type project is the Global Database of Events, Language and Tone (GDELT), a worldwide, multidecade, geo-referenced, daily event dataset. The GDELT monitors print, broadcast, and news media sources in over 100 languages, across every country in the world, using machine translation technology to access non-English sources. The aim of the project is to catalog human, societal-scale behaviors down to a micro-level. For example, it can use dozens of data fields to capture all available details about a particular event such as a small terrorist attack, the individual actors involved, and their roles.[314] The Institute for the Study of Violent Groups has developed another example with a database containing detailed information on some 223,000 incidents of violent extremism and transnational crime involving over 43,000 unique individuals with connections to over 3,000 violent groups. This dataset is based on traditional media, social media, video content, police reports, and court documents, among other sources. The database structure contains as many as 1,500 variables to help categorize individual events then visualize the linkages within the data.[315]

Some far reaching "big data" applications eventually may offer improved methods for predictive analysis going beyond the targeting of individuals already identified as threats. For example, they may be able to provide a means to screen preemptively specific actors or highlight environmental conditions that are more likely to produce radicalization among certain individuals. For instance, the Global Terrorism Database project at the University of Maryland contains detailed records of some 125,000 terrorist incidents dating back to the 1970s, using 40 to 120 variables for each incident record.[316] From within this repository, researchers have developed a more detailed dataset of some 1,500 people radicalized toward violent and nonviolent extremism in the United States since World War II, including biographic information, criminal records, social networks, and personal histories. This data has enabled researchers to identify some important commonalities among the group including the importance of social networks and presence of key facilitators, but also variables such as age, marital status, and proxy measures for social assimilation.

While critics charge that the promise of big data has been perpetually oversold, it likely offers one of the few viable alternatives for refining risk profiling models and behavioral indicators linked to identity-based screening, as well as potentially supporting strategies for preemptive interventions before social alienation moves individual actors toward radicalization and violence. See the following scenario.

As the investigation continued, the analysis of the suspect's social media network provided dozens of investigative leads in the United States and several European countries. Linkages confirmed the suspect's involvement with other actors known to be part of a foreign fighter facilitation network responsible for recruiting and moving new fighters to an initial entry point in Syria for indoctrination and training. These leads prompted several preemptive interventions focused on individuals already in the recruitment pipeline. Exploitation of additional photos and content derived from social media posts provided evidence that narrowed down the possible location of the Syrian training site and identified several other individuals operating at the location. Based on the subject's operational profile and significant evidence of personal connections to the foreign fighter network, the UK government filed criminal charges against the individual and initiated a formal extradition request with Turkish authorities.

ASSESSING IWAR 1.0

The preceding scenario and discussion surveyed just a small portion of the emerging technology landscape and considered how these tools may be used for the waging of iWar in the future. This exploration was speculative rather than predictive, acknowledging the uncertain course of technology innovation and the highly dynamic nature of the threat environment. These factors highlight the enormous challenges facing military planners and policymakers as they attempt to align defense strategy with research and development goals focused on the most likely, and pressing, future risks to U.S. national security.

In this sense, the story of iWar may be read as a cautionary tale concerning the hazards of misplaced prediction of future threats and the technologies needed to defeat them. Much of what has been described in this monograph evolved not as a matter of premeditated design, but rather from a decade of ad hoc adaptations in response to exigencies created by an unexpected adversary. This situation required that the U.S. national security apparatus quickly reorient on a new kind of threat, then develop supporting doctrines, technologies, and methods needed to meet these challenges.

The ability of the military, intelligence community, and domestic security entities to recognize what was needed and eventually put these plans into action is a testimony to the ingenuity and dedication of these organizations and individuals. However, it also highlights the enormous cost and risk of making the wrong decision. As the U.S. Army's operating concept points out:

> thinking clearly about future armed conflict requires consideration of threats, enemies and adversaries, anticipated missions, emerging technologies, opportunities to use existing capabilities in new ways, and historical observations and lessons learned.[317]

Even under the best of circumstances, this represents a formidable task.

In assessing the larger significance of iWar, a few definitions should be clarified. The term "warfare" describes the way in which nations make war, specifically the tools, techniques, and methods of applying coercive power against an adversary on the battlefield. Extending from this, the "character of war" describes this phenomenon of warfare contextualized within a larger milieu of cultural, technological, social, political, and bureaucratic influences. The rise of iWar reflects a significant change on both levels of analysis.

As a new model of warfare, iWar formed a distinct set of tools, techniques, and methods that evolved over a relatively short period of time from theory into practice in direct response to specific operational challenges on the battlefield. These challenges primarily centered on the task of fighting an adversary organized as networks and the operational need to identify, screen, and target the individual combatants within these networks. In this sense, iWar represents something truly unique about the changing character of modern war, specifically the phenomena of individual, named combatants becoming legitimate objects of state warfare and the focus of operational targeting.

The larger question remains as to whether this operational paradigm represents a fundamental and enduring shift in how America organizes, equips, and wages such conflicts in the future. Alternately, this episode may simply represent a transient diversion from the national security establishment's traditional focus on conventional, maneuver-style warfare waged against state-based adversaries. The answer to this question implies a larger issue of whether or not the United States will return to a model of warfare where, once again, combatants are anonymous agents on the battlefield, targeted on the basis of status rather than identity. At this point, the answer to this question is not entirely obvious.

FUTURE IWAR AS POLICY AND STRATEGY: CAUTIONS AND CONSIDERATIONS

In the weeks following the attacks of 9/11, the United States embarked upon a conflict for which it was largely ill-prepared. The military had spent the decades of the Cold War developing doctrines and technologies geared for the prospect of major conventional force engagement against state-based adversaries. The ambiguity of the security environment during the 1990s did little to alter the powerful force of inertia or divert the national security establishment from this relatively narrow strategic focus.

However, the rise of disruptive, nonstate actors such as al-Qaeda and the experience of two protracted counterinsurgency campaigns brought about a fundamental shift in how national security decisionmakers viewed the principal threats to U.S. interests. The response to these new threats involved major structural, technical, and functional transformations undertaken in the midst of conflict. As a result, the United States ultimately developed a ruthlessly effective operational-level capability for identifying and targeting small cells and individual combatants across the battlefield. It was equally successful in applying these techniques toward focused counterterrorism targeting across a wider expanse of ungoverned spaces and locations where local security forces were either unable or unwilling to engage these threats.

On the domestic front, the United States leveraged similar technologies and information management tools in support of identity-based screening strategies that have kept borders, transportation networks, and American citizens remarkably safe since 9/11. However, at the same time, these remarkable tactical and technical achievements have not fully delivered desired political end-states at the strategic level. This is particularly true with regard to stabilizing volatile regions and stemming the perpetual regeneration of individual threats emerging from such places as Afghanistan, Iraq, Yemen, Somalia, Syria, and Libya.

These setbacks arguably have altered American strategic calculus, possibly for generations. As the President's most recent National Security Strategy emphasizes, America has shifted away from a strategy based on fighting costly, large-scale ground wars in lieu of:

> a more sustainable approach that prioritizes targeted counterterrorism operations, collective action with responsible partners, and increased efforts to prevent the growth of violent extremism and radicalization that drives increased threats.

Yet, even with these words of restraint, the President emphasized that:

> outside of areas of active hostilities, we endeavor to detain, interrogate, and prosecute terrorists through law enforcement. However, when there is a continuing, imminent threat, and when capture or other actions to disrupt the threat are not feasible, we will not hesitate to take decisive action.[318]

In word and deed the current administration has suggested that many of the foundational pillars of the iWar paradigm will continue to play a part of U.S. strategic approaches. However, this also suggests a national security strategy that will primarily focus on risk mitigation rather than military victory. This may be a strategy that does not offer any clear political end-state other than the immediate tactical goal of identifying and neutralizing the most pressing threats to key U.S. interests and citizens. If that is the case, then this will be a conflict waged primarily with information rather than conventional weapons, emphasizing technical tools and cognitive skills more than firepower and maneuver. This mode of warfare will continue to strain the traditional bureaucratic boundaries and functional separations between law enforcement, military actions, and intelligence activities. As one commentator recently observed, the nature of these modern security threats "makes it virtually impossible to draw neat lines between war and peace, foreign and domestic, emergency and normality."[319] As this mode of warfare becomes normalized, it is also likely to challenge accepted privacy norms, perhaps with significant implications for the larger issue of identity and how it relates to national security.

In concluding this monograph, a few cautions and recommendations are offered. First, it must be kept in mind that iWar evolved primarily as a strategy of tactics. It represented methods and tools designed to treat symptoms but not the disease. The doctrinal and technical innovations of iWar dealt with a very specific operational challenge of identifying, screening and targeting network-based adversaries and individual combatants. However, it has very little to offer in terms of dealing with the underlying causes of instability and political violence. For this reason, the methods of iWar must be applied with circumspection and in a manner that does not conflate targeting with strategy. General McMaster has cautioned against this "raiding mentality" and the fallacy that strategic victories can be achieved simply by identifying critical network nodes, then eliminating them with surgical precision. A related concern is that, as the United States demonstrates increasing prowess in these methods, it will produce overconfidence in technologies of iWar. This caution stems from a very consistent American predilection for techno-scientific solutions to every national security problem, even when these repeatedly fail to fulfill their initial promise. A decade of refining these methods has clearly demonstrated an important place for technologies that "remove a violent extremist's greatest defense—anonymity;" however, the utility of these tools must not be oversold.[320]

Regardless of future strategic choices, the innovations resulting from a decade of waging iWar have produced extraordinary capabilities at the operational and tactical levels. These skills, tools, and methods must continue to mature even as persistent operational demands subside. This includes the recent doctrinal, technical, organizational, and policy innovations that have been central to waging this mode of warfare. By all indications, various forms of hybrid war and irregular threats will persist into the near future. This will inevitably involve U.S. military activities in ungoverned spaces, with weak identity regimes and adversaries determined to use anonymity for operational advantage. Therefore, the need for identity verification on the battlefield and on borders will not diminish.

In terms of doctrine innovation, there is a great risk of stagnation, from the Army in particular, as military forces gravitate back toward traditional focus on conventional force engagement against state-based adversaries. iWar, as waged over the last decade, will remain an inherently land force-centric mode of warfare. It cannot be fought from the air and will remain dependent upon ground forces for useful intelligence gathering and performing effective targeting. For this reason, the emerging doctrines of identity intelligence and identity operations must continue to mature and be integrated into a flexible concept of full spectrum military operations.

Among the major technical challenges will be detecting and exploiting a range of nonstandard signatures and data sources (cyber, open source, social media, biometrics, and forensics) and integrating these with conventional collection streams for improved situational awareness. This will require continued improvements in areas such as standoff biometric collection and expeditionary forensics, as well as advances in data integration and information sharing between the defense, intelligence, and homeland security communities. This will demand new methods for data processing and analytical tools designed for dealing with large amounts of unstructured information—all representing enormous technical challenges that cannot wait for the next crisis.

In terms of organizational change, it is time to acknowledge that current and future threats will continue to erode the distinctions between external defense and internal security. An individual of interest encountered in a combat zone may also have relevance to a customs agent at John F. Kennedy Airport, New York, a police officer conducting a routine stop in Tucson, Arizona, or a counterterrorism analyst at the CIA. Bureaucratic interests, technical barriers, and over-classification must not inhibit robust information sharing among these entities. This realization should inform a more deliberate process to reconfigure the national security apparatus with seamless integration as the basic organizing principle. However, this discussion must also include a re-evaluation of the legal and policy frameworks to ensure appropriate protections of information, as well as necessary checks on power in order to address civil liberty and privacy concerns.

At the outset, this analysis noted how the iWar paradigm has challenged fundamental aspects of the

Westphalia construct, including many of the legal foundations that have defined the conduct of state warfare in the modern age. Over the last decade, the United States has demonstrated a remarkable tactical proficiency at waging this kind of warfare, particularly the identification, screening, and targeting of individual combatants around the globe. However, the continuing debates over disposition of detainees held in Guantanamo, Cuba, acrimony over the scope and application of the AUMF, and lingering concerns over nonbattlefield lethal targeting all suggest that many of the issues regarding the conduct of iWar remain unresolved, if not controversial.

If the United States continues to operate under the premise that threats posed by individual combatants now represent a significant national security concern and, therefore, are a legitimate object of state warfare, then there must be a corresponding legal and ethical framework guiding how this kind of war will be waged. In order to be effective, this construct must have equivalent scope and authority as existing structures that have defined the terms and limits of conventional conflict for decades. For America, this is a particularly salient need. As the world's remaining superpower, its security must rest upon unquestioned legitimacy in the use of military force no matter the choice of strategy, tools, or methods.

ENDNOTES

1. Sun Tzu, *The Art of War*, Thomas Cleary, trans., Boston, MA: Shambhala Pocket Classics, 1991.

2. Micah Zenko, "The U.S. Just Launched Its 500th Drone Strike," *Defense One*, November, 21, 2014, available from *www. defenseone.com/threats/2014/11/us-just-launched-its-500th-drone-*

strike/99722/?oref=defenseone_today_nl. Also, the New American Foundation, *Long War Journal*, and Bureau of Investigative Journalism all monitor U.S. drone strikes taking place outside the "active combat zones" of Iraq, Afghanistan, and Libya. The 500 total strikes in Pakistan, Yemen, and Somalia represent an average among the range of estimates from these organizations as of November 2014. This number includes a total of seven U.S. citizens killed by drone strikes during the Obama administration.

3. Jo Becker and Scott Shane, "Secret 'Kill List' Proves a Test of Obama's Principles and Will," *The New York Times*, May 29, 2012.

4. Linda Robinson, Paul D. Miller, John Gordon IV, Jeffrey Decker, Michael Schwille, and Raphael S. Cohen, *Improving Strategic Competence: Lessons from 13 Years of War*, Santa Monica, CA: RAND, 2014, p. 26.

5. John Arquilla and David Ronfeldt, *Networks and Netwars: The Future of Terror, Crime, and Militancy*, Santa Monica, CA: RAND, 2001.

6. Thomas L. Friedman, *The Lexus and the Olive Tree*, New York: Anchor Books, 2000.

7. Arquilla and Ronfeldt.

8. Defense Science Board Task Force on Defense Intelligence, *Counterinsurgency: Intelligence, Surveillance, and Reconnaissance Operations*, Washington, DC: Office of the Under Secretary of Defense for Acquisition, Technology, and Logistics, February 2011, p. 52.

9. Martin van Creveld, *The Rise and Decline of the State*, New York: Cambridge University Press, 1999, pp. 162-163.

10. Jean-Jacques Rousseau, "The Social Contract," Victor Gourevitch, ed., *The Social Contract and Other Writings*, New York: Cambridge University Press, 1997, p. 51.

11. Gabriella Blum, "The Individualization of War: From War to Policing in the Regulation of Armed Conflicts," Austin Sarat, Lawrence Douglas, and Martha Merrill Umphrey, eds., *Law and War: An Introduction*, Redwood City, CA: Stanford University Press, 2014, p. 52.

12. For elaboration on this concept, see Gabriella Blum, "The Dispensable Lives of Soldiers," *Journal of Legal Analysis*, Vol. 2, No. 1, Spring 2010, pp. 115-147.

13. 10 U.S.C. § 948a: US Code, Section 948A defines "unprivileged enemy belligerent" as an individual (other than a privileged belligerent) who (A) has engaged in hostilities against the United States or its coalition partners; (B) has purposefully and materially supported hostilities against the United States or its coalition partners; or (C) was a part of al Qaeda at the time of the alleged offense under this chapter.

14. Samuel Issacharoff and Richard Pildes, "Targeted Warfare: Individuating Enemy Responsibility," *New York University Law Review*, Vol. 88, No. 5, November 2013, p. 1,521.

15. In addition to dozens of journal articles on this topic, see "Forensics and Warrant Based Targeting," March 2010, Ft. Leavenworth, KS: Center for Army Lessons Learned (CALL), for a detailed discussion of how this concept has been applied operationally.

16. van Creveld, p. 163.

17. There are certainly exceptions to this rule in American history, notably targeting against such figures as Poncho Villa, Hitler, Yamamoto, Gadhafi, Noriega, Mohammed Aideed, and Osama Bin Laden. However, as a practical matter prior to 9/11, leadership targeting was generally applied as a discrete military objective that was adjunct to the larger political purpose of the conflict. As such, it has not been a central feature of warfighting strategies or formalized as part of doctrinal approaches until recently.

18. Benjamin Rhodes, Deputy National Security Advisor, from an interview with NPR. Quote reprinted in Bill Chappell, "U.S. Won't Rule Out Attack In Syria To Hit Islamic State," August 21, 2014, available from *www.npr.org/blogs/thetwo-way/2014/08/21/342165273/u-s-won-t-rule-out-attack-in-syria-to-hit-islamic-state*.

19. Rosa Brooks, "There's No Such Thing as Peacetime," *Foreign Policy*, March 13, 2015, available from *www.foreignpolicy. com/2015/03/13/theres-no-such-thing-as-peacetime-forever-war-terror-civil-liberties/*.

20. John Abizaid and Rosa Brooks, *Recommendations and Report of the Task Force on US Drone Policy*, Washington, DC: Stimson Center, June 2014, p. 12.

21. Among others, see recent discussions on this topic by Issacharoff and Pildes, and Gabriella Blum.

22. U.S. Joint Chief of Staff, Joint and Coalition Operational Analysis Division (J7), *Decade of War Volume 1: Enduring Lessons from the Past Decade of Operations*, Washington, DC: U.S. Joint Chiefs of Staff, June 15, 2012, p. 2.

23. U.S. Department of the Army, *Field Manual* (FM) *3-60, The Targeting Process*, Washington, DC: Headquarters, Department of the Army, November 26, 2010, p. B-1.

24. Office of the Under Secretary of Defense for Acquisition, Technology, and Logistics, *Report of the Defense Science Board Task Force on Defense Biometrics*, Washington, DC: Defense Science Board, March 2007.

25. General David Petraeus, Commander, U.S. Central Command, Multi-National Force-Iraq, "Counterinsurgency Guidance," June 21, 2008.

26. Targeting doctrine defines "high-value individuals," or HVIs, as "persons of interest (friendly, adversary, or enemy) who must be identified, surveilled, tracked, and influenced through the use of information or fires." See FM 3-60, p. B-1.

27. Christopher J. Lamb and Evan Munsing, *Secret Weapon: High-Value Target Teams as an Organizational Innovation*, Washington, DC: National Defense University Press, March 2011, p. 33.

28. Stanley McChrystal, "It Takes a Network: The New Front Line of Modern Warfare," *Foreign Policy*, February 21, 2011, available from *www.foreignpolicy.com/2011/02/21/it-takes-a-network/*.

29. Carlotta Gall, "Night Raids Curbing Taliban, but Afghans Cite Civilian Toll," *The New York Times*, July 8, 2011. Also see Tom Peter, "Afghanistan: NATO's Night Raids Cause More Harm than Good, Report Says," *The Christian Science Monitor*, September 19, 2011.

30. Charles Faint and Michael Harris, "F3EAD: Ops/Intel Fusion Feeds The SOF Targeting Process," *Small Wars Journal*, January 31, 2012.

31. U.S. Joint Forces Command, *Commander's Handbook for Attack the Network*, Suffolk, VA: Joint Warfighting Center, Joint Doctrine Support Division, May 20, 2011.

32. Steve Ressler, "Social Network Analysis as an Approach to Combat Terrorism: Past, Present and Future Research," *Homeland Security Affairs*, Vol. 2, No. 2, July 2006.

33. See Duncan Watts, *Six Degrees: The Science of a Connected Age*, New York: W. W. Norton, 2003; and *Small Worlds: The Dynamics of Networks between Order and Randomness*, Princeton, NJ: Princeton University Press, 1999.

34. Ajay Mehra, Daniel Brass, Giuseppe Labianca, and Stephen Borgatti, "Network Analysis in the Social Sciences," *Science*, Vol. 323, No. 5916, February 13, 2009, pp. 892-895.

35. *FM 3-24, Counterinsurgency*, Washington, DC: Headquarters, Department of the Army, December 15, 2006, Appendix B.

36. John A. Nagl, "The Evolution and Importance of Army/Marine Corps Field Manual 3-24, Counterinsurgency," Foreword to the U.S. Army/Marine Corps Counterinsurgency Field Manual by the United States Army and United States Marine Corps, Chicago, IL: University of Chicago Press, 2007, available from *www.press.uchicago.edu/Misc/Chicago/841519foreword.html*.

37. For useful analysis on the integration of SNA into the Army's counterinsurgency doctrine, see David Knoke, "It Takes a Network: The Rise and Fall of Social Network Analysis in U.S. Army Counterinsurgency Doctrine," and John A. Nagl, "Constructing the Legacy of Field Manual 3-24," *Joint Forces Quarterly*, Vol. 58, pp. 118-120.

38. FM 3-24, Appendix B.

39. FM 3-60, p. B-1.

40. Bob Woodward, "Why Did Violence Plummet? It Wasn't Just the Surge," *The Washington Post*, September 8, 2008, available from *www.washingtonpost.com/wp-dyn/content/article/2008/09/07/AR2008090701847.html*.

41. *Joint Publication* (JP) *3-24, Counterinsurgency*, Washington, DC: U.S. Joint Chiefs of Staff, November 2013, p. XVI.

42. Joint Center for Operational Analysis, *Operation IRAQI FREEDOM, January 2007 to December 2008 The Comprehensive Approach: An Iraq Case Study*, Norfolk, VA: U.S. Joint Forces Command, February 2010, p. 14.

43. See *Army Electronic Publication* (ATP) *2-33.4 Intelligence Analysis*, August 2014, JP 2.01-3 *Joint Intelligence Preparation of the Operational Environment*, June 2009, and FM 3-60.

44. Some critics remain skeptical with regard as to how fully the military has embraced these ideas and whether they still influence thinking about future warfighting concepts, particularly as many leaders advocate a return to conventional warfighting approaches and doctrines. See Knoke for this contrasting viewpoint.

45. See United States Marine Corps (USMC) *IdOps Strategy 2020* and U.S. Department of the Navy, *Marine Corps Order 5530.17, Marine Corps Identity Operations* (IdOps), November 13, 2012.

46. *Ibid.*

47. Anthony Smith and Mark Schaefer, "More Than Just Biometrics: Why Marine Corps Identity Operations are Critical to MAGTF Mission Success," *Marine Corps Gazette*, Vol. 98, No. 5, May 2014.

48. Identity intelligence (I2) appeared for the first time as part of recognized doctrine in October 2013 in the updated version of JP 2.0, *Joint Intelligence*, then more recently in the latest version of

JP 3-05, *Special Operations*, July 2014, where it described I2 as "the collection, analysis, exploitation, and management of identity attributes and associated technologies and processes."

49. JP 3-26, *Counterterrorism,* Washington, DC: U.S. Joint Chiefs of Staff, October 24, 2014, p. V-5.

50. Robert O. Work and Shawn Brimley, *20YY: Preparing for War in the Robotic Age*, Washington, DC: Center for a New American Security, 2014, p. 17.

51. Antoine Bousquet, "Cyberneticizing the American War Machine: Science and Computers in the Cold War," *Cold War History*, Vol. 8, No. 1, 2008.

52. Emily Mushen and Jonathan Schroden, *Are we Winning? A brief History of Military Operations Assessment*, Washington, DC: CNA Center for Stability and Development, 2014.

53. Charles Shrader, *History of Operations Research in the U.S. Army, Volume III, 1973-1995*, Washington, DC: Office of the Deputy Under Secretary of the Army for Operations Research, 2009.

54. William Westmoreland, "Address to the Association of the U.S. Army," October 14, 1969, cited in Antoine Bousquet, *Cybernetic Warfare: Computers and the Cold War*, Meeting of International Studies Association, San Diego, CA, March 22, 2006.

55. Robert Tomes, "The Cold War Offset Strategy: Assault Breaker and the Beginning of the RSTA Revolution," *War on the Rocks Blog*, November 20, 2014, available from *www.warontherocks. com/2014/11/the-cold-war-offset-strategy-assault-breaker-and-the-beginning-of-the-rsta-revolution/*.

56. Mark Mazzetti, *The Way of the Knife*, New York: Penguin Books, 2014, pp. 94-101. Also see Andrew Callam, "Drone Wars: Armed Unmanned Aerial Vehicles," *International Affairs Review*, Vol. XVIII, No. 3, Winter 2010.

57. Jeremiah Gertler, *U.S. Unmanned Aerial Systems*, Washington, DC: Congressional Research Service, January 3, 2012.

58. Amitai Etzioni, "The Great Drone Debate," *Military Review*, Vol. 93, No. 2, March-April 2013, p. 2.

59. Andrew Callam, "Drone Wars: Armed Unmanned Aerial Vehicles," *International Affairs Review*, Vol. XVIII, No. 3, Winter 2010.

60. Abizaid and Brooks, p. 11. Unclassified reporting suggests a significant increase in the use of such strikes during the Obama administration with 33 strikes in 2008 and 54 in 2009, killing at least 20 militant leaders. See Simon Frankel Pratt, "Crossing off Names: The Logic of Military Assassination," *Small Wars and Insurgencies*, Vol. 26, No. 1, pp. 3-24.

61. Pratt.

62. Bill Roggio, "U.S. Military Confirms it Killed Islamic State, Shabaab Leaders in Airstrikes," *Long War Journal Blog*, February 11, 2015, available from *www.longwarjournal.org/archives/2015/02/us_military_confirms.php#ixzz3RWChIqr]*.

63. Micah Zenko, *Reforming U.S. Drone Strike Policies*, Washington, DC: Council on Foreign Relations, January 2013, p. 8.

64. U.S. Department of Defense, *Defense Science Board Task Force on COIN and ISR Operations*, Washington, DC: Office of the Undersecretary of Defense for Acquisition, Technology, and Logistics, February 2011, p. 65.

65. Office of the Under Secretary of Defense for Acquisition, Technology, and Logistics, "Report of the Defense Science Board Task Force on Defense Biometrics," Washington, DC: Defense Science Board, March 2007, p. 39.

66. Anthony Iasso, "A Critical Time for Biometrics and Identity Intelligence," *Military Intelligence Professional Bulletin*, July-September 2013, pp. 39-40.

67. Timothy S. McWilliams and Nicholas J. Schlosser, "U.S. Marines in Battle: Fallujah," November-December 2004, Quantico, VA: U.S. Marine Corps, 2014, p. 62. Also see Thom Shanker, "To Track Militants, U.S. Has System That Never Forgets a Face,"

The New York Times, July 13, 2011, available from *www.nytimes.com/2011/07/14/world/asia/14identity.html?_r=0*.

68. Jody Kieffer and Kevin Trissell, "DOD Biometrics: Lifting the Veil of Insurgent Identity," *Army AT&L Magazine*, April-June 2010, pp. 14-17, available from *asc.army.mil/docs/pubs/alt/2010/2_AprMayJun/articles/14_DOD_Biometrics--Lifting_the_Veil_of_Insurgent_Identity_201002.pdf*.

69. Myra Gray, "Defending the U.S. with Biometrics," *Infosecurity*, Vol. 6, No. 6, September/October 2009, pp. 24–25.

70. Spencer Ackerman, "U.S. Holds on to Biometric Database of 3 Million Iraqis," *Wired Magazine, Danger Room Blog*, December 21, 2011, available from *www.wired.com/2011/12/iraq-biometrics-database/*.

71. *Additional Training for Leaders and More Timely Transmission of Data Could Enhance the Use of Biometrics in Afghanistan*, Washington, DC: U.S. Government Accountability Office, April 2012, p. 1.

72. David Pendall and Cal Sieg, "Biometric-Enabled Intelligence in Regional Command–East," *Joint Forces Quarterly*, Vol. 72, No. 1, January 2014, p. 70.

73. U.S. Army, *Commander's Guide to Biometrics in Afghanistan: Observations, Insights, and Lessons*, Ft. Leavenworth, KS: Center for Army Lessons Learned, April 2011. Also see *Additional Training for Leaders and More Timely Transmission of Data Could Enhance the Use of Biometrics in Afghanistan*, p. 8.

74. "Biometrics in Afghanistan: The Eyes Have It," *The Economist*, July 7, 2012, available from *www.economist.com/node/21558263*.

75. For a useful overview discussion of the issues and summary of various recidivism rate estimates, see Jennifer Elsea and Michael John Garcia, "Wartime Detention Provisions in Recent Defense Authorization Legislation," Washington, DC: Congressional Research Service, January 23, 2015, pp. 14-16.

76. Martin Chulov, "ISIS: The Inside Story," *The Guardian*, December 11, 2014, available from *www.theguardian.com/world/2014/dec/11/-sp-isis-the-inside-story*.

77. David Axe, "CSI Somalia: Interpol Targets Pirates," *Wired Magazine, Danger Room Blog,* June 18, 2009, available from *www.wired.com/2009/06/csi-somalia-interpol-targets-pirates/*.

78. Antonia Greene, "Including Biometrics in Deployment Training Helps Soldiers Identify the Enemy," *U.S. Army Office of Public Affairs,* 174th Infantry Brigade, April 30, 2012, available from *www.army.mil/article/78894/Including_biometrics_in_deployment_training_helps_Soldiers_identify_the_enemy*.

79. Deputy Secretary of Defense, *Authority to Collect, Store, and Share Biometric Information of Non-U.S. Persons with U.S. Government (USG) Entities and Partner Nations,* Memorandum, Washington, DC, January 12, 2012.

80. VIBES, Leidos Product Publication, available from *www.leidos.com/products/software/vibes*.

81. Erik Bowman, "Game Changers in DoD Biometrics," conference presentation at the 2012 Biometric Consortium, September 20, 2012, Tampa, FL, available from *www.biometrics.org/bc2012/presentations/Workshops/SS_Thur_900-1000a_Game%20Changers_Bowman.pdf*.

82. U.S. Marine Corps, *Marine Corps Forensic Enterprise Strategy,* April 20, 2010, p. 3, available from *www.mccdc.marines.mil/Portals/172/Docs/SWCIWID/SWAAB/IW%20Reader/MCFES_Final%20%2020%20April.pdf*.

83. *Additional Planning and Oversight Needed to Establish an Enduring Expeditionary Forensic Capability,* Washington, DC: U.S. Government Accountability Office, June 2013, p. 4.

84. Oliver Herion, "Expeditionary Forensic Support to Joint Force Commanders: What Changes or Considerations are Warranted?" Quantico, VA: U.S. Marine Corps Command and Staff College, April 2012, p. v.

85. Douglas Shontz, *DNA as Part of Identity Management for the Department of Defense,* Santa Monica, CA: RAND, 2010, p. 7.

86. Michael Johnston, "Expeditionary Forensics: The Warrior's Science Revealing the Hidden Enemy," *Military Police*, Spring 2009, pp. 5-7.

87. "U.S. Used Lab in Afghanistan to Confirm bin Laden's DNA," *Associated Press*, August 30, 2013, available from *www.spokesman.com/stories/2013/aug/30/in-brief-us-used-lab-in-afghanistan-to-confirm*.

88. Patrick Tucker, "Special Operators are Using Rapid DNA Readers," *Defense One*, May 21, 2015, available from *www.defenseone.com/technology/2015/05/special-operators-are-using-rapid-dna-readers/113383/?oref=defenseone_today_nl*.

89. Marine Corps Forensic Enterprise Strategy, p. 5.

90. *Additional Planning and Oversight Needed to Establish an Enduring Expeditionary Forensic Capability*, p. 1.

91. Joop Voetelink, "EvBO: Evidence-Based Operations, How to Remove the Bad Guys from the Battlefield," *Journal of International Law of Peace and Armed Conflict*, Vol. 4, 2013, p. 195.

92. Thomas B. Smith and Marc Tranchemontagne, "Understanding the Enemy: The Enduring Value of Technical and Forensic Exploitation," *Joint Forces Quarterly*, Vol. 75, No. 4, October 2014, p. 124.

93. Anthony Iasso, "A Critical Time for Biometrics and Identity Intelligence," *Military Intelligence Professional Bulletin*, July-September 2013, pp. 39-40.

94. United States Government Accountability Office, "Defense Forensics: Additional Planning and Oversight Needed to Establish an Enduring Expeditionary Forensic Capability," June 2013, available from *www.gao.gov/assets/660/655546.pdf*.

95. Sandra I. Erwin, "As Defense, Intelligence Agencies Drown in Data, Technology Comes to the Rescue," *Nation Defense Magazine*, November 2014.

96. Stephen Mayhew, "U.S. Defense Department Biometrics Database Upgraded," DoD Press Release, as reported in *Biometrics*

Update, December 16, 2014, available from *www.biometricupdate. com/201412/u-s-defense-department-biometrics-database-upgraded* and *www.dote.osd.mil/pub/reports/FY2013/pdf/army/2013dodabis.pdf.*

97. Patrick Tucker, "Jihadi John and the Future of the Biometrics Terror Hunt," *Defense One*, February 27, 2015, available from *www.defenseone.com/technology/2015/02/jihadi-john-and-future-biometrics-terror-hunt/106263/?oref=defenseone_today_nl.*

98. Siobhan Gorman, "How Team of Geeks Cracked Spy Trade," *The Wall Street Journal*, September 4, 2009, available from *www.wsj.com/articles/SB125200842406984303.*

99. Andy Greenberg and Ryan Mac, "How A 'Deviant' Philosopher Built Palantir, A CIA-Funded Data-Mining Juggernaut," *Forbes*, August 14, 2013, available from *www.forbes.com/sites/ andygreenberg/2013/08/14/agent-of-intelligence-how-a-deviant-philosopher-built-palantir-a-cia-funded-data-mining-juggernaut/.*

100. George I. Seffers, "Army's Talking Technology," *Signal Magazine*, September 2011, available from *www.afcea.org/ content/?q=armys-talking-technology.*

101. Erik Bowman, "Game Changers in DoD Biometrics," and "Biometric Data Storage and Biometric Intelligence," presentations at the 2013 Biometrics Big Data Symposium For Defense, Intelligence, Homeland Security and Law Enforcement, June 18, 2013, Washington, DC, p. 11, available from *www.semanticcommunity.info/@api/deki/files/27723/Bowman-TTC_Biometric_BigData_Conf_fl13.pdf.*

102. For a useful recent overview, see Lisa Seghetti, "Visa Waiver Program," William L. Painter, ed., *Selected Issues in Homeland Security Policy for the 114th Congress,* Washington, DC: Congressional Research Service, May 2015, pp. 38-41.

103. Alison Siskin, *Visa Waiver Program*, Washington, DC: Congressional Research Service, February 2014, pp. 5-8.

104. "FBI Announces Biometrics Suite's Full Operational Capability," FBI Press Release, September 23, 2014, available from *www.fbi.gov/news/stories/2014/september/fbi-announces-biometrics-*

suites-full-operational-capability/fbi-announces-biometrics-suites-full-operational-capability.

105. Aliya Sternstein, "Homeland Security To Roll Out Biometrics Along the Border This Summer," *Defense One*, January 28, 2015, available from *www.defenseone.com/technology/2015/01/homeland-security-roll-out-biometrics-along-bordersummer/103968/?o ref=defenseone_today_nl*. Also see "OBIM Wants Info on Biometric Matching Systems," *PlanetBiometrics*, April 28, 2015, available from *www.planetbiometrics.com/article-details/i/2981/desc/obim-wants -info-on-biometric-matching-systems/*, accessed April 29, 2015. See more at *www.planetbiometrics.com/article-details/i/2981/desc/obim-wants-info-on-biometric-matching-systems/#sthash.qFSOtHkQ.dpuf*.

106. Amanda Vicinanzo, "Vulnerabilities in Coast Guard's Biometric System May Impede Identification of Suspected Terrorists," *Homeland Security Today*, March 14, 2015, available from *www.hstoday.us/briefings/daily-news-analysis/single-article/vulnera-bilities-in-coast-guards-biometric-system-may-impede-identification-of-suspected-terrorists/bc0e386816bcc3e25b64ebcbd7ee3309.html*.

107. Stephen Mayhew, "Obama's New National Security Strategy Makes a Push for Biometrics Data Sharing," *Biometric Update*, February 10, 2015, available from *www.biometricupdate. com/201502/obamas-new-national-security-strategy-makes-a-push-for-biometrics-data-sharing*.

108. This information includes, but is not limited to, biometric data: finger scans and digital facial photographs; encounter data: place and date of visa issuance; and biographic data: name, date of birth, gender, physical details, and visa issuance or visa refusal data.

109. The Consular Consolidated Database (CCD). For a complete discussion, see Ruth Ellen Wasem, *Immigration: Visa Security Policies*, Washington, DC: Congressional Research Service, June 2014, p. 6.

110. Wasem.

111. Kathleen Kiernan, "Counterintelligence and Law Enforcement," Jennifer Sims and Burton Gerber, eds., *Vaults, Mirrors*

& Masks: Rediscovering U.S. Counterintelligence, Washington, DC: Georgetown University Press, 2009, p. 159.

112. John Wagner, Written testimony of CBP Office of Field Operations Acting Deputy Assistant Commissioner John Wagner for a House Committee on Oversight and Government Reform, Subcommittee on National Security hearing titled "Border Security Oversight, Part III: Border Crossing Cards and B1/B2 Visas," November 14, 2013, available from *www.dhs.gov/news/2013/11/14/ written-testimony-cbp-house-oversight-and-government-reform-sub-committee-national.*

113. Currently, citizens of 38 countries may travel to the United States without a visa as part of the Visa Waiver Program based on the 2007 *Homeland Security Presidential Directive 6* legislation. For a useful discussion, see a recent post on the Lawfare blog by Nathan Sales, "Is the Visa Waiver Program a Threat to our National Security?" February 2, 2015, available from *www.lawfareblog.com/2015/02/is-the-visa-waiver-program-a-threat-to-our-national-security/.*

114. Martin Rudner, "Intelligence-Led Air Transport Security: Pre-Screening for Watch-Lists, No-Fly Lists to Forestall Terrorist Threats," *International Journal of Intelligence and Counterintelligence,* Vol. 28, No. 1, 2015, p. 48.

115. National Counterterrorism Center, *Terrorist Identities Datamart Environment* (TIDE) *Factsheet,* August 2014, available from *www.nctc.gov/docs/tidefactsheet_aug12014.pdf.*

116. Adam Goldman, "More than 1 Million People are Listed in U.S. Terrorism Database," *The Washington Post,* August 5, 2014, available from *www.washingtonpost.com/world/national-security/more-than-1-million-people-are-listed-in-us-terrorism-data-base/2014/08/05/a66de30c-1ccc-11e4-ab7b-696c295ddfd1_story.html.*

117. *Ibid.*

118. Ken Kroupa, "An Inside Look at DoD's DNA," presentation delivered at the 2010 Biometrics Consortium, September 21-23, 2010, Tampa, FL, available from *www.biometrics.org/bc2010/ presentations/RapidDNA/kroupa-An-Inside-Look-at-DoD-s-DNA.pdf.*

119. "Report of the Defense Science Board Task Force on Defense Biometrics," p. 31.

120. FBI CODIS: National DNA Index (NDIS), FBI Homepage, available from *www.fbi.gov/about-us/lab/biometric-analysis/codis/ndis-statistics*.

121. Gefrides and Welch.

122. Patrick Tucker, "Special Operators are Using Rapid DNA Readers," *Defense One*, May 21, 2015, available from *www.defenseone.com/technology/2015/05/special-operators-are-using-rapid-dna-readers/113383/?oref=defenseone_today_nl*.

123. Thomas B. Smith and Marc Tranchemontagne, "Understanding the Enemy: The Enduring Value of Technical and Forensic Exploitation," *Joint Forces Quarterly*, Vol. 75, Fall 2014, pp. 122-128.

124. "Next Generation Identification, FBI Announces Biometrics Suite's Full Operational Capability," FBI Press Release, September 23, 2014, available from *www.fbi.gov/news/stories/2014/september/fbi-announces-biometrics-suites-full-operational-capability/fbi-announces-biometrics-suites-full-operational-capability*.

125. Robert Schroeder, "A Strategic Evolution: A Path to Border Security," *Holding the Line in the 21st Century*, Washington, DC: U.S. Customs and Border Protection, p. 38.

126. Justin Lee, "Customs' Facial Recognition Technology Trial Raises Privacy Concerns," *Biometric Update*, May 29, 2015, available from *www.biometricupdate.com/201505/customs-facial-recognition-technology-trial-raises-privacy-concerns*.

127. *Authorization for the Use of Military Force* (AUMF), Joint Resolution 23, 107th Cong., 1st sess., September 14, 2001. Also see Public Law § 2(a), 115 Stat, p. 224.

128. John O. Brennan, "The Efficacy and Ethics of U.S. Counterterrorism Strategy," public remarks delivered at the Wilson Center, April 30, 2012, available from *www.wilsoncenter.org/event/the-efficacy-and-ethics-us-counterterrorism-strategy*.

129. John Yoo, "Assassinations or Targeted Killings since 9/11," *New York Law School Review*, Vol. 57, 2011, p. 63.

130. According to recent polling, while Americans generally are concerned over government surveillance, some 82 percent say it is acceptable to monitor communications of suspected terrorists. For details of recent polling, see Lee Rainie and Mary Maddens, "Americans' Privacy Strategies Post-Snowden," Pew Research Center, March 16, 2015, available from *www.pewinternet.org/2015/03/16/americans-privacy-strategies-post-snowden/.* For public opinion on drone strikes, see Sarah Kreps, "Do Americans Really Love Drone Strikes?" *The Washington Post,* June 6, 2014.

131. George W. Bush, *Homeland Security Presidential Directive* (HSPD-6, *Directive on Integration and Use of Screening Information To Protect Against Terrorism*), September 16, 2003, available from *www.gpo.gov/fdsys/pkg/PPP-2003-book2/pdf/PPP-2003-book2-doc-pg1174.pdf.*

132. George W. Bush, *Directive on Biometrics for Identification and Screening to Enhance National Security,* June 5, 2008, available from *www.gpo.gov/fdsys/pkg/PPP-2008-book1/pdf/PPP-2008-book1-doc-pg757.pdf.* Also see DoD *Instruction on Defense Biometric and Forensic Enabled Intelligence* (DoD O-3300.bb), directing DoD to make available to other U.S. Government agencies, to the fullest extent permitted by law, all biometric and associated information on persons posing a threat to national security. Biometric data collected by DoD is integrated into the Automated Biometric Identification System (ABIS) and shared with the Department of Homeland Security, FBI, and various elements of the intelligence community.

133. Dennis C. Blair, Senate Select Committee on Intelligence, *U.S. Intelligence Community Annual Threat Assessment 2010*, February 3, 2010, available from *www.dni.gov/files/documents/Newsroom/Testimonies/20100203_testimony.pdf.*

134. Steve Coll, "The Unblinking Stare: The Drone War in Pakistan," *The New Yorker*, November 24, 2014.

135. One recent notable example was the January 2015 drone strike that accidentally killed two hostages held by al-Qaeda, one

of them an American. Similar strikes also killed two Americans who were reportedly members of al-Qaeda, Ahmed Farouq and Adam Gadahn, who were not specifically targeted as part of the operation. See Peter Baker and Julie Hirschfeld Davis, "2 Qaeda Hostages Were Accidentally Killed in U.S. Strike, White House Says," *The New York Times*, April 23, 2015, available from *www. nytimes.com/2015/04/24/world/asia/2-qaeda-hostages-were-accidentally-killed-in-us-raid-white-house-says.html?hp&action=click&pgtype=Homepage&module=span-ab-top-region&region=top-news&WT.nav=top-news*.

136. Patrick Tucker, "How Special Operators Are Taking Artificial Intelligence To War," *Defense One*, May 28, 2015, available from *www.defenseone.com/technology/2015/05/how-special-operators-are-taking-artificial-intelligence-war/113872/?oref=defenseone_today_nl*.

137. Danya Greenfield, "The Case Against Drone Strikes on People Who Only 'Act' Like Terrorists," *The Atlantic*, August 19, 2013. Also see *Civilian Casualties & Collateral Damage* at the Brookings Institute Lawfare Blog, available from *www.lawfareblog.com/wiki/the-lawfare-wiki-document-library/targeted-killing/controversy*.

138. Greg Miller, "Plan for Hunting Terrorists Signals U.S. Intends to Keep Adding Names to Kill Lists," *Washington Post*, October 23, 2012.

139. Comment by Micah Zenko, a scholar at the Council on Foreign Relations and the lead author of a 2013 study of drone warfare. See Scott Shane, "Drone Strikes Reveal Uncomfortable Truth: U.S. is Often Unsure About Who Will Die," *The New York Times*, April 23, 2015, available from *www.nyti.ms/1JiGHtY*.

140. See Brennan, "The Efficacy and Ethics of U.S. Counterterrorism Strategy." Also, one recent example of this policy was the capture of a "top al-Qaeda operative" and American citizen, Muhanad Mahmoud al Farekh, in Pakistan, who was reportedly nominated to the Pentagon's "kill list" of suspected terrorists in 2013; however, he was captured by Pakistani forces and secretly flown to the United States to face federal terrorism charges. See Adam Goldman and Tim Craig, "American Citizen Linked to al-Qaeda is Captured, Flown Secretly to U.S.," *The Washington Post*, April 2, 2015, available from *www.washingtonpost.com/*

world/national-security/american-citizen-suspected-of-being-al-qae-
da-member-captured-brought-to-us/2015/04/02/48e8cc4c-d89c-11e4-
8103-fa84725dbf9d_story.html.

141. Christopher Lamb and Evan Munsing, *Secret Weapon: High-Value Target Teams as an Organizational Innovation,* Washington, DC: Institute for National Strategic Studies, National Defense University, 2011, p. 53.

142. Tom Peter, "In Iraq, Troops Balance Fighting and Lending a Hand," *The Christian Science Monitor,* August 7, 2008, available from *www.csmonitor.com/World/Middle-East/2008/0807/p06s 01-wome.html.*

143. Gabriella Blum, "The Individualization of War: From War to Policing in the Regulation of Armed Conflicts," Sarat, Douglas, and Umphrey, eds., *Law and War,* Stanford, CA: Stanford University Press, 2013, available from *www.ssrn.com/abstract=2231168.*

144. For a useful discussion of World War II as a "scientists' war," see Paul Kennedy, *Engineers of Victory: The Problem Solvers who Turned the Tide in the Second World War,* New York: Random House, 2013.

145. See articles on personality identification playing cards, available from *www.defenselink.mil/news/Apr2003/pipc10042003. html*; and Tom Zucco, "Troops Dealt an Old Tool," *St. Petersburg Times,* April 12, 2003, available from *www.sptimes.com/2003/04/12/ Worldandnation/Troops_dealt_an_old_t.shtml.*

146. Sydney J. Freedberg, "Raiders, Advisors and the Wrong Lessons from Iraq," *Breaking Defense,* March 20, 2013, available from *www.breakingdefense.com/2013/03/gen-mcmaster-raiders-advisors-and-the-wrong-lessons-from-iraq.*

147. Barrack Obama, "Remarks by the President at the National Defense University, Speech at the National Defense University, May 23, 2013, transcript available from *www.whitehouse. gov/the-press-office/2013/05/23/remarks-president-national-defense-university.*

148. Adam Grissom, "The Future of Military Innovation Studies," *The Journal of Strategic Studies*, Vol. 29, No. 5, October 2006, p. 907.

149. For one perspective on this distinction, see Stephen Rosen, *Winning the Next War: Innovation and the Modern Military*, Ithica, NY: Cornell University Press, 1991.

150. President Barack Obama, Interview on Fareed Zakaria GPS, February 1, 2015, transcript available from *transcripts.cnn.com/TRANSCRIPTS/1502/01/fzgps.01.html*.

151. Patrick Tucker, "What Happens When Spies Can Eavesdrop on Any Conversation?" *Defense One*, December 1, 2014, available from *www.defenseone.com/technology/2014/12/what-happens-when-spies-can-eavesdrop-any-conversation/100142/?oref=defenseone_today_nl*.

152. Jim Garamone, "Capabilities Must Match Future Threats, Army Leader Says," *DoD News, Defense Media Activity*, February 24, 2015, available from *www.defense.gov/news/newsarticle.aspx?id=128237*.

153. U.S. National Intelligence Council, *Global Trends 2030: Alternative Worlds*, Washington, DC: U.S. Director of National Intelligence, December 2012, pp. 59–60.

154. Matthew G. Olsen, Director of the National Counterterrorism Center, Hearing before the Senate Committee on Homeland Security, "Worldwide Threats to the Homeland," September 17, 2014, available from *www.nctc.gov/docs/2014_worldwide_threats_to_the_homeland.pdf*.

155. Howard Altman, "Experience Briefing President Leads New Agency Chief to Raise Bar," *The Tampa Tribune*, November 14, 2014, available from *www.tbo.com/list/military-news/experience-briefing-president-leads-new-agency-chief-to-raise-bar-20141114*.

156. *Global Trends 2030*, p. 50.

157. Ken Dilanian, "20,000 Foreign Fighters Flock to Syria, Iraq," *Associated Press*, February 10, 2015, available from *news.*

yahoo.com/ap-exclusive-20-000-foreign-fighters-flock-syria-211811073. html.

158. Eric Schmitt and Michael Schmidt, "West Struggles to Halt Flow of Citizens to War Zones," *The New York Times*, January 13, 2015, available from *www.nytimes.com/2015/01/13/world/west-struggles-against-flow-to-war-zones.html.*

159. "Report on Foreign Terrorist Fighters," New York: United Nations, March 2015, pp. 14-23.

160. *Ibid.*, pp. 18-23.

161. Greg Miller, "Backlash in Berlin Over NSA Spying Recedes as Threat from Islamic State Rises," *The Washington Post*, December 29, 2014, available from *www.washingtonpost.com/world/national-security/backlash-in-berlin-over-nsa-recedes-as-islamic-state-rises/2014/12/29/c738af28-8aad-11e4-a085-34e9b9f09a58_story.html.*

162. Ahmed Rashid, "Waking Up to the New al-Qaeda," *New York Review of Books*, January 12, 2015, available from *www.nybooks.com/blogs/nyrblog/2015/jan/12/paris-attacks-waking-al-qaeda.*

163. John Mueller and Mark Stewart, "How French Intelligence Missed the Charlie Hebdo Terrorists," *Time*, January 14, 2015, available from *www.time.com/author/john-mueller-and-mark-stewart.*

164. Alissa J. Rubin, "Lawmakers in France Move to Vastly Expand Surveillance," *The New York Times*, May 5, 2015, available from *www.nytimes.com/2015/05/06/world/europe/french-legislators-approve-sweeping-intelligence-bill.html?_r=0.*

165. An expression coined by NATO officials and first used during the 2014 Crimean crisis, referring to masked Russian soldiers and military equipment within Ukraine.

166. Assessment by the International Institute for Strategic Studies (IISS) in the annual *Military Balance* report, see Radio Free Europe/Radio Liberty, "Report Warns Russia's Hybrid Warfare In Ukraine Could Inspire Others," February 11, 2015, available from *www.rferl.org/content/russia-hybrid-warfare-ukraine-could-inspire-others/26842566.html.*

167. Agence France-Press, "French Soldiers In Mali Stalked By Invisible Enemy," May 30, 2015, available from *www.defnews. ly/1HCvUFn.*

168. Patrick Tucker, "What Happens When Spies Can Eavesdrop on Any Conversation?" *Defense One*, December 1, 2014, available from *www.defenseone.com/technology/2014/12/what-happens-when-spies-can-eavesdrop-any-conversation/100142/.*

169. Elizabeth Young, "Summary of the "Decade of War," *Prism*, Vol. 4, No. 2, 2013, p. 126.

170. Alan Gelb and Julia Clark, "Identification for Development: The Biometrics Revolution," Washington, DC: Center for Global Development, January 2013, p. 7.

171. "UN begins biometric registration of Rwandans in DRC," *Planet Biometrics*, April 13, 2015, available from *www.planetbiometrics.com/article-details/i/2905/.*

172. Justin Lee, "UNHCR, Accenture Provide Global Biometric Identity Management System to Help Refugees," *Biometric Update*, May 25, 2015, available from *www.biometricupdate.com/201505/unhcr-accenture-provide-global-biometric-identity-management-system-to-help-refugees.*

173. Jennifer Hicks, "United Nations High Commissioner For Refugees Adopts Biometric Tracking," *Forbes*, May 31, 2015, available from *www.forbes.com/sites/jenniferhicks/2015/05/30/united-nations-high-commissioner-for-refugees-adopts-biometric-tracking/.*

174. Rosa Brooks, "Know Thy Enemy, and the Future of Memorial Day," *Foreign Policy*, May 25, 2015, available from *www.foreignpolicy.com/2015/05/25/drones-dna-facebook-future-war-memorial-day/.*

175. Charles J. Dunlap, Jr., "The Hyper-Personalization of War: Cyber, Big Data, and the Changing Face of Conflict," *Georgetown Journal of International Affairs*, Vol. 15, 2014, pp. 108-118.

176. Estimate based on a recent technology market research report by ABI Research. See Anna Forrester, "Commercial Segment to Overtake Government in Biometrics Spending by 2017,"

ExecutiveBiz Blog, February 11, 2015, available from *www.blog.ex-ecutivebiz.com/2015/02/abi-research-commercial-segment-to-overtake-govt-in-biometrics-spending-by-2017/*.

177. Justin Lee, "U.S. Government Biometrics Spend to Reach US$8.6 B by 2020: ABI Research," *Biometrics Update*, April 20, 2015, available from *www.biometricupdate.com/201504/u-s-government-biometrics-spend-to-reach-us8-6-b-by-2020-abi-research*.

178. Zack Martin, "Goode Predicts Mobile Biometric Growth," *Secure ID News*, February 4, 2014, available from *www.secure-idnews.com/news-item/goode-predicts-mobile-biometric-growth/#*. Article references the monthly industry report by Goode Intelligence entitled, "Fingerprint Biometrics and Mobile and Wearable Biometrics."

179. Gelb and Clark.

180. "Government and technology: Playing leapfrog: The Wonders of Smart Systems," *The Economist*, May 24, 2015, available from *www.economist.com/node/21651330/print*.

181. UK Home Office, Guidance Notes, "Biometric Residence Permits, General Information for Applicants, Employers and Sponsors," March 2015, available from *www.gov.uk/government/uploads/system/uploads/attachment_data/file/413959/v_4_BRP_-_Generic_information_leaflet_2_March_-_6_April__clean_.pdf*.

182. "Nigerian Communications Commission Deploys BIO-Key Fingerprint Technology for National SIM Card Registration Program," *Marketwired*, May 28, 2013, available from *www.finance.yahoo.com/news/nigerian-communications-commission-deploys-bio-120000546.html*.

183. Tim Craig and Shaiq Hussain, "Pakistanis Face a Deadline: Surrender Fingerprints or Give up Cellphone," *The Washington Post*, February 23, 2015, available from *www.washingtonpost.com/world/asia_pacific/pakistanis-face-a-deadline-surren-der-fingerprints-or-give-up-cellphone/2015/02/23/de995a88-b932-11e4-bc30-a4e75503948a_story.html?utm_source=Sailthru&utm_medium=email&utm_term=%2ASituation%20Report&utm_campaign=Sit%20Rep%20February%2025%202015*.

184. Paul Roderick Gregory, "Putin's New Weapon In The Ukraine Propaganda War: Internet Trolls," *Forbes*, December 9, 2014, available from *www.forbes.com/sites/paulroderickgregory/2014/12/09/putins-new-weapon-in-the-ukraine-propaganda-war-internet-trolls/*.

185. *Department of Defense Cyber Strategy*, Washington, DC: U.S. Government Printing Office, April 2015, p. 12.

186. Linda Kinstler, "Global Cyber Defense Demand Will Exceed Capability for Years To Come," *Defense One*, January 28, 2015, available from *www.defenseone.com/technology/2015/01/global-cyber-defense-demand-will-exceed-capability-years-come/103983/*.

187. Chris White, "New Search Engine Exposes the Dark Web," Interview with CBS 60 Minutes with the DARPA developer on a new technology for searching internet "dark web" sites, February 8, 2015, available from *www.cbsnews.com/news/new-search-engine-exposes-the-dark-web*.

188. Tor, or The Onion Routing project, was originally developed by the U.S. Naval Research Laboratory for the purpose of protecting government communications and is now used by a wide variety of private and commercial interests. For a discussion of the potential for anonymous use of Bitcoin, see Craig Elwell, Maureen Murphy, and Michael Seitzinger, *Bitcoin: Questions, Answers, and Analysis of Legal Issues*, Washington, DC: Congressional Research Service, January 28, 2015, p. 3.

189. Mark Wallace, Written Testimony before the House Committee on Foreign Affairs Subcommittee on Terrorism, Nonproliferation, and Trade, "The Evolution of Terrorist Propaganda: The Paris Attack and Social Media," January 27, 2015, available from *www.counterextremism.com/press/counter-extremism-project-ceo-mark-wallace-testify-house-committee-foreign-affairs*.

190. Tim Fernholz, "Terrorism Finance Trackers Worry ISIS Already Using Bitcoin," February 13, 2015, *Defense One*, available from *www.defenseone.com/threats/2015/02/terrorism-finance-trackers-worry-isis-already-using-bitcoin/105345/?oref=defenseone_today_nl*.

191. Patrick Tucker, "How the Military Will Fight ISIS on the Dark Web," February 24, 2015, *Defense One*, available from *www. defenseone.com/technology/2015/02/how-military-will-fight-isis-dark-web/105948/?oref=defenseone_today_nl*.

192. National Intelligence Council, *Global Trends 2030: Alternative Worlds*, Washington, DC: National Intelligence Council, December 2012, p. 128, available from *www.dni.gov/files/documents/ GlobalTrends_2030.pdf*.

193. Matthew G. Olsen, Hearing before the Senate Committee on Homeland Security, "Worldwide Threats to the Homeland," September 17, 2014.

194. Gabriel Weimann, *New Terrorism and New Media*, Washington, DC: Commons Lab of the Woodrow Wilson International Center for Scholars, 2014, p. 1.

195. Michael Chertoff and Tobby Simon, "The Impact of the Dark Web on Internet Governance and Cyber Security: Global Commission on Internet Governance Paper Series No. 6," Waterloo, Ontario, Canada: Centre for International Governance Innovation and the Royal Institute for International Affairs, February 2015, p. 1.

196. Patrick Tucker, "What Your Facebook Posts Mean to U.S. Special Operations Forces," *Defense One*, January 29, 2015, available from *www.defenseone.com/technology/2015/01/what-your-face-book-posts-mean-usspecialforces/104031/?oref=defenseone_today_nl*.

197. Marc Lynch, Deen Freelon, and Sean Aday, "Syria's Socially Mediated Civil War," *Peaceworks*, No. 91, January 2014, available from *www.usip.org/sites/default/files/PW91-Syrias%20So-cially%20Mediated%20Civil%20War.pdf*.

198. Weimann, p. 2; and Haroro Ingram, "Three Traits of the Islamic State's Information Warfare," *The RUSI Journal*, Vol. 159, No. 6, 2004, pp. 4-11.

199. J. M Berger and Jonathon Morgan, *The ISIS Twitter Census: Defining and Describing the Population of ISIS Supporters on Twitter*, Analysis Paper No. 20, Washington, DC: Brookings Project

on U.S. Relations with the Islamic World, March 2015, p. 2. Also see Brian Bennett, "With Islamic State Using Instant Messaging Apps, FBI Seeks Access to Data," *The Los Angeles Times*, June 10, 2015, available from *www.latimes.com/world/middleeast/la-fg-terror-messaging-20150608-story.html#page=1 1/5.*

200. Joseph Carter, Shiraz Maher, and Peter Neumann, *#Greenbirds: Measuring the Importance and Influence of Foreign Fighter Networks,* London, UK: The International Centre for the Study of Radicalization and Political Violence, April 2014, available from *www.icsr.info/wp-content/uploads/2014/04/ICSR- Report-Greenbirds-Measuring-Importance-and-Infleunce-in-Syrian-Foreign-Fighter-Networks.pdf.*

201. Joe Parkinson and Maria Abi-Habib, "How Jihadists Slip Through Europe's Dragnet and Into Syria," *The Wall Street Journal,* February 20, 2015, available from *www.wsj.com/articles/how-jihadists-slip-through-europes-dragnet-and-into-syria-1424653670.*

202. Julian Barnes, "U.S. Military Plugs into Social Media for Intelligence Gathering," *The Wall Street Journal,* August 6, 2014, available from *www.wsj.com/articles/u-s-military-plugs-into-social-media-for-intelligence-gathering-1407346557.*

203. James Rupert, "Russian Troops Lead Moscow's Biggest Direct Offensive in Ukraine Since August," January 23, 2015, *Atlantic Council,* available from *www.atlanticcouncil.org/blogs/new-atlanticist/russian-special-forces-and-regular-troops-lead-moscow-s-biggest-direct-offensive-in-ukraine-since-august.*

204. Daniel Regalado, Nart Villeneuve, and John Scott Railton, *Behind the Syrian Conflict's Digital Front Lines,* Milpitas, CA: Firefly Inc., February 2015, p. 5.

205. *Behind the Syrian Conflict's Digital Front Lines,* p. 18.

206. Brian Everstine, "Carlisle: Air Force Intel Uses ISIS 'Moron's' Social Media Posts to Target Airstrikes," *Air Force Times,* June 4, 2015, available from *www.airforcetimes.com/story/military/tech/2015/06/04/air-force-isis-social-media-target/28473723/.*

207. See "The ISIS Twitter Census," as one recent example.

208. "Anonymous 'Hacktivists' Strike a Blow against ISIS," Anonymous website, available from *www.anonhq.com/anonymous-hacktivists-strike-blow-isis*.

209. David Sanger and Eric Schmitt, "Hackers Use Old Lure on Web to Help Syrian Government," *The New York Times*, February 1, 2015, available from *www.nytimes.com/2015/02/02/world/middleeast/hackers-use-old-web-lure-to-aid-assad.html?_r=0*.

210. Generically, "OPSEC" refers to a process that identifies one's own critical information and determines if it can be obtained by adversaries and exploited for their use. It also includes the use of measures that eliminate or reduce these risks.

211. Johann Wolfgang von Goethe, *Maxims and Reflections*, Bailey Saunders, trans., New York: The MacMillan Company, 1906, available from *onlinebooks.library.upenn.edu/webbin/gutbook/lookup?num=33670*.

212. Charles J. Dunlap, Jr., "The Hyper-Personalization of War: Cyber, Big Data, and the Changing Face of Conflict," Vol. 15, *Georgetown Journal of International Affairs*, 2014, p. 113.

213. Michael Shear and Scott Shane, "White House Weighs Sanctions after Second Breach of a Computer System," *The New York Times*, June 12, 2015, available from *www.nytimes.com/2015/06/13/us/white-house-weighs-sanctions-after-second-breach-of-a-computer-system.html?hp&action=click&pgtype=Homepage&module=first-column-region&_r=0*.

214. Patrick Radden Keeke, "Rocket Man: How an Unemployed Blogger Confirmed that Syria had Used Chemical Weapons," *The New Yorker*, November 25, 2013, available from *www.newyorker.com/magazine/2013/11/25/rocket-man-2*.

215. The same individual involved in the Syrian chemical weapons reporting also founded Bellingcat, a forum for citizen investigative journalism with a focus on military and security issues. See *www.bellingcat.com*.

216. Paul Rosenzweig, *Cyberwarfare: How Conflicts in Cyberspace are Challenging America and Changing the World*, Santa Barbara, CA: ABC-CLIO, 2013, p. 20.

217. Weimann, p. 10.

218. Patrick Tucker, "What Happens When You Pose as the Defense Secretary on Twitter?" *Defense One*, December 2, 2014, available from *www.defenseone.com/technology/2014/12/what-hap pens-when-you-pose-next-defense-secretary-twitter/100304/.*

219. Bruce Schneier, "Hacker or Spy? In Today's Cyberattacks, Finding the Culprit is a Troubling Puzzle," *The Christian Science Monitor*, March 4, 2015, available from *www.csmonitor.com/ World/Passcode/Passcode-Voices/2015/0304/Hacker-or-spy-In-today-s-cyberattacks-finding-the-culprit-is-a-troubling-puzzle.*

220. Greg Miller, "CIA Looks to Expand its Cyber Espionage Capabilities," *The Washington Post*, February 23, 2015, available from *www.washingtonpost.com/world/national-security/ cia-looks-to-expand-its-cyber-espionage-capabilities/2015/02/23/ a028e80c-b94d-11e4-9423-f3d0a1ec335c_story.html?utm_ source=Sailthru&utm_medium=email&utm_term=%2ASituation%20 Report&utm_campaign=Sit%20Rep%20February%2025%202015.*

221. Carl von Clausewitz, *On War*, Michael Howard and Peter Paret, eds. and trans., Princeton, NJ: Princeton University Press, 1976, p. 595.

222. For doctrinal discussion on this issue, see *JP 5-0, Joint Operation Planning*, Chap. III, "Operational Art and Operational Design," August 11, 2011.

223. Mary Madden and Lee Rainie, "Americans' Attitudes about Privacy, Security, and Surveillance," Pew Research Center, May 20, 2015, available from: *www.pewinternet.org/2015 /05/20/ americans-attitudes-about-privacy-security-and-surveillance/.*

224. *Ibid.* Some 69 percent of adults say they are not confident that records of their activity maintained by the social media sites they use will remain private and secure, while only 9 percent say they feel they have "a lot" of control over how much information is collected about them and how it is used.

225. Sydney Freedberg, "6 Threats, 6 Changes, & A Brave New World: Intel Chief Vickers," *Breaking Defense*, January 21, 2015, available from *www.breakingdefense.com/2015/01/6-threats-6-changes-a-brave-new-world-intel-chief-vickers.*

226. Brian Barrett, "Can Google's Future-Lab Finally Kill the Password?" *Wired*, May 29, 2015, available from *www.wired. com/2015/05/google-atap-passwords-vault-io/*.

227. Evelyn Brown, *Performance of Facial Recognition Software Continues to Improve*, Washington, DC: National Institute of Standards and Technology, June 3, 2014, available from *www.nist.gov/ itl/iad/face-060314.cfm*. Data based on a research study conducted by Patrick Grother and Mei Ngan, "Performance of Face identification Algorithms."

228. Andrea Peterson, "The Biometrics Revolution is Already Here—and You May Not be Ready For It," *The Washington Post*, October 17, 2014, available from *www.washingtonpost.com/blogs/ the-switch/wp/2014/10/17/the-biometrics-revolution-is-already-here-and-you-may-not-be-ready-for-it*.

229. Yaniv Taigman, Ming Yang, Marc'Aurelio Ranzato, and Lior Wolf, "DeepFace: Closing the Gap to Human-Level Performance in Face Verification," Facebook Research Publication, Menlo Park, CA and Tel Aviv University, Tel Aviv, Israel, 2014, available from *https://research.facebook.com/ publications/480567225376225/deepface-closing-the-gap-to-human-level-performance-in-face-verification/*. Also see Tom Simonite, "Facebook Creates Software That Matches Faces Almost as Well as You Do," *MIT Technology Review*, March 17, 2014, available from *www.technologyreview.com/news/ 525586/facebook-creates-software-that-matches-faces-almost-as-well-as-you-do/*, accessed January 7, 2015.

230. National Science and Technology Council (NSTC) Committee on Homeland and National Security, Subcommittee on Biometrics, *Introduction to Biometrics*, pp. 129-130, available from *www.biometrics.gov/ReferenceRoom/Introduction.aspx*.

231. Major distorting factors are referenced by the acronym, APIER—aging, pose, illumination, expression, and resolution.

232. Patrick Grother and Mei Ngan, "Face Recognition Vendor Test: Performance of Face Identification Algorithms," Washington, DC: Department of Commerce, National Institute of Standards and Technology, May 26, 2014, available from *www.nist. gov/customcf/get_pdf.cfm?pub_id=915761*.

233. Stephan Mracek, Jan Vana, Radim Dvorak, and Svetlana Yanushkevich, "3D and Thermo-Face Fusion," Jucheng Yang and Shan Juan Xie, eds., *New Trends and Developments in Biometrics, Intech,* November 28, 2012, available from *www.intechopen.com/ books/new-trends-and-developments-in-biometrics.*

234. Erik Sofge, "The End of Anonymity," *Popular Science,* January 15, 2014, available from *www.popsci.com/article/technology/ end-anonymity.*

235. While not exclusively useful for identification purposes, physiological characteristics and thermal markers might be employed for screening individuals suspected of having certain medical issues, fever, etc.

236. Babak Hodjat, "Myth Busting Artificial Intelligence," *Wired Magazine,* February 19, 2015, available from *www.wired.com/ insights/2015/02/myth-busting-artificial-intelligence/.*

237. Robert Hof, "Deep Learning," *MIT Technology Review,* April 23, 2013, available from *www.technologyreview.com/featured- story/513696/deep-learning.*

238. Quentin Hardy, "Facebook Offers Artificial Intelligence Tech to Open Source Group," January 16, 2015, *The New York Times,* available from *bits.blogs.nytimes.com/2015/01/16/facebook- offers-artificial-intelligence-tech-to-open-source-group/.*

239. Jose Pagliery, "FBI Launches a Face Recognition System," *CNN.com,* September 16, 2014, available from *www.money. cnn.com/2014/09/16/technology/security/fbi-facial-recognition.*

240. "The Face Detection Algorithm Set To Revolutionize Image Search," *MIT Technology Review,* February 16, 2015, referencing the paper by Sachin Sudhakar Farfade, Mohammad Saberian, and Li-Jia Li, "Multi-view Face Detection Using Deep Convolutional Neural Networks," February 10, 2015, available from *www. arxiv.org/abs/1502.02766.*

241. James Albers, "The Truth about Biometric Exit Technology," *Security Today,* October 1, 2014, available from *www. security-today.com/articles/2014/10/01/the-truth-about-biometric-exit.*

aspx. StereoVision recently demonstrated a Wireless 3D Binocular Face Recognition System in response to a Navy contract for technologies focused on "stand-off identification of uncooperative subjects." See Patrick Tucker, "The Navy's New Binoculars Can Identify You From 700 Feet Away," *Defense One*, May 15, 2015.

242. Alex Hern, "Hacker Fakes German Minister's Fingerprints," *The Guardian*, December 30, 2014, available from *www.theguardian.com/technology/2014/dec/30/hacker-fakes-german-ministers-fingerprints-using-photos-of-her-hands*.

243. Peter Counter, "New Iris Innovations May Bring Eye-Based Biometrics to the Masses," *Mobile ID World*, January 15, 2015, available from *www. mobileidworld.com/new-iris-innovations-may-bring-eye-based-biometrics-to-the-masses-1151*.

244. Sean Lyngaas, "Can the Pentagon Keep Pace on Biometrics?" *FCW.com*, March 11, 2015, available from *fcw.com/Articles/2015/03/11/Can-the-Pentagon-keep-pace-on-biometrics.aspx?m=2&p=1*.

245. *Ibid.*

246. Federal Bureau of Investigation, "Image-Based Matching Technology Offers Identification and Intelligence Prospects," FBI Press Release, December 2012, available from *https://www.fbi.gov/about-us/cjis/cjis-link/december-2012/Image-Based%20Matching%20Technology%20Offers%20Identification%20and%20Intelligence%20Prospects*.

247. Douglas Reynolds, "Speaker Verification: From Research to Reality," Paper presented at the 2002 Institute of Electrical and Electronics Engineers (IEEE), International Conference Acoustics, Speech, and Signal Processing, May 13-17, 2002, available from *www.ll.mit.edu/mission/cybersec/publications/publication-files/full_papers/020513_Reynolds.pdf*.

248. Taylor Haney, *The Future of Voiceprints*, Los Angeles, CA: Annenberg Media Center, December 27, 2014, available from *www.neontommy.com/news/2014/12/future-voiceprints*.

249. Patrick Tucker, "What Happens When Spies Can Eavesdrop on Any Conversation?" *Defense One*, December 1, 2014,

available from *www.defenseone.com/technology/2014/12/what-happens-when-spies-can-eavesdrop-any-conversation/100142/*.

250. Homayoon Beigi, "Speaker Recognition: Advancements and Challenges," Jucheng Yang and Shan Juan Xie, eds., *New Trends and Developments in Biometrics, Intech*, November 28, 2012, available from *www.intechopen.com/books/new-trends-and-developments-in-biometrics*.

251. NSTC, Committee on Homeland and National Security, Subcommittee on Biometrics, *Introduction to Biometrics*, pp. 129-130, available from *www.biometrics.gov/ReferenceRoom/Introduction.aspx*.

252. VIBES Product Information Sheet from the Leidos Corporation, Reston, VA, available from *www.leidos.com/sites/default/files/files/14-0439vFc-VIBES_FS.pdf*.

253. Rachel Metz, "Deep Learning Squeezed onto a Phone," *MIT Technology Review*, February 9, 2015, available from *www.technologyreview.com/news/534736/deep-learning-squeezed-onto-a-phone*.

254. Ray Locker, "Military Could Be Using High-Tech Speech Software by 2017," *USA Today*, February 22, 2015, available from *www.usatoday.com/story/news/nation/militaryintelligence/2015/02/22/robust-speech-translation-transcription-software/23839041/*.

255. "Laboratory Team Takes Honors at the 2014 Audio/Visual Emotion Challenge and Workshop," *MIT Lincoln Laboratory, The Bulletin*, January 9, 2015.

256. Chuck Brooks, "Human Factors and Biometrics at DHS," *Biometric Update*, August 1, 2014, available from *www.biometricupdate.com/201408/human-factors-and-biometrics-at-dhs*.

257. DARPA, Detection & Computational Analysis of Psychological Signals Information Sheet, May 2013, available from *www. webcache.googleusercontent.com/search?q=cache:mM_FJrE2m7oJ:www.darpa.mil/opencatalog/DCAPShtml+&cd=2&hl=en&ct=clnk&gl=us*.

258. Norberto Andradejun, "Computers Are Getting Better Than Humans at Facial Recognition," *The Atlantic*, June 9, 2014, available from *www.theatlantic.com/technology/archive/2014/06/bad-news-computers-are-getting-better-than-we-are-at-facial-recognition/372377*.

259. Roman Yampolskiy and Venu Govindaraju, "Behavioral Biometrics: A Survey and Classification," *International Journal of Biometrics*, Vol. 1, No. 1, 2008, p. 81.

260. *Ibid.*, p. 88.

261. Julian Barnes, "U.S. Military Plugs into Social Media for Intelligence Gathering, Defense Intelligence Agency Head Says Online Postings Played Crucial Role in Ukraine Jet Shootdown," *The Wall Street Journal*, August 6, 2014, available from *www.wsj.com/articles/u-s-military-plugs-into-social-media-for-intelligence-gathering-1407346557*.

262. Peter Counter, "Behavioral Biometrics to Become Increasingly Standard in Fraud Detection," *FindBiometrics*, July 23, 2014, available from *www.findbiometrics.com/behavioural-biometrics-to-become-increasingly-standard-in-fraud-detection*.

263. Boer Deng, "People Identified through Credit-Card Use Alone," *Nature*, January 29, 2015, available from *www.nature.com/news/people-identified-through-credit-card-use-alone-1.16817*.

264. For one recent example of these applications, see patent filing for Israeli behavioral biometrics firm BioCatch. Related article available from "BioCatch Granted Behavioural Biometric Patent for Mobiles," *Planet Biometrics*, February 25, 2015, available from *www.planetbiometrics.com/article-details/i/2746*.

265. James Vincent, "Behaviosec uses Behavioral Biometrics to Find If the Person Using a Mobile Device Is Really Who They Claim to Be," *The Independent*, September 2, 2014, available from *www.economictimes.indiatimes.com/news/international/business/behaviosec-uses-behavioural-biometrics-to-find-if-the-person-using-a-mobile-device-is-really-who-they-claim-to-be/articleshow/41463585.cms*.

266. Aliya Sternstein, "NSA Trying to Track Your Smartphone Finger Strokes," *Defense One*, May 26, 2015, available from *www.defenseone.com/technology/2015/05/nsa-trying-track-your-smartphone-finger-strokes/113638/??oref=d_brief_nl*.

267. Yedid Hoshen and Shmuel Peleg, "Egocentric Video Biometrics," Jerusalem, Israel: The Hebrew University of Jerusalem, November 27, 2014, available from Cornell University Library at *www.arxiv.org/pdf/1411.7591v1.pdf*.

268. Rachel Metz, "Deep Learning Squeezed onto a Phone," *MIT Technology Review*, February 9, 2015, available from *www.technologyreview.com/news/534736/deep-learning-squeezed-onto-a-phone/*.

269. Yampolskiy and Govindaraju, p. 93.

270. D. A. Reid, S. Samangooei, C. Chen, M. S. Nixon, and A. Ross, "Soft Biometrics for Surveillance: An Overview," C. R. Rao and Venu Govindaraju, eds., *Handbook of Statistics*, Vol. 31, Oxford, UK: Elsevier, 2013.

271. Daniel Reid and Mark Nixon, "Imputing Human Descriptions in Semantic Biometrics," paper presented at the Multimedia in Forensics, Security and Intelligence conference, Florence, Italy, October 2010, available from *eprints.soton.ac.uk/271623/1/mifor541-reid.pdf*.

272. J. Thornton, J. Baran-Gale, D. Butler, M. Chan, and H. Zwahlen, "Person Attribute Search For Large-Area Video Surveillance," IEEE Conference on Technologies for Homeland Security, 2011, available from *ieeexplore.ieee.org/xpl/login.jsp?tp=&arnumber=6107847&url=http%3A%2F%2Fieeexplore.ieee.org%2Fstamp%2Fstamp.jsp%3Ftp%3D%26arnumber%3D6107847*.

273. The probability that two unrelated individuals would share all 13 pairs of alleles used in the FBI's n 13 core short tandem repeat (STR) profile is estimated to be one in several hundred billion. See Nathan James, "DNA Testing in Criminal Justice: Background, Current Law, Grants, and Issues," Washington, DC: Congressional Research Service, December 6, 2012, p. 3.

274. Another method involves the use of mitochondrial DNA (mtDNA) sequencing that is useful for evidence samples such as hair fragments, bones, and teeth. This analysis is highly sensitive and therefore can be used in cases with limited biological material or degraded samples. However, because mtDNA profiles are only shared between maternal family members, this method is not as discriminating as STR analysis for identification.

275. Lisa Gefrides and Katie Welch, "Forensic Biology: Serology and DNA," Ashraf Mozayani and Carla Noziglia, eds., *The Forensic Laboratory Handbook Procedures and Practice*, New York: Springer, 2011, p. 28.

276. DNA Casework Unit (DCU) Information Page, FBI website, available from *www.fbi.gov/about-us/lab/biometric-analysis/dna-casework-unit-dcu-1*.

277. FBI Rapid DNA or Rapid DNA Analysis, FBI homepage, available from *www.fbi.gov/about-us/lab/biometric-analysis/codis*.

278. Kathy Pretz, "New System to Speed Up DNA Analysis," *The Institute*, February 4, 2013, available from *theinstitute.ieee.org/technology-focus/technology-topic/new-system-to-speed-up-dna-analysis*. For a technical description, see Melissa May, "Field-Deployable Rapid DNA Analysis: Fully Integrated, Fully Automated Generation of Short Tandem Repeat Profiles of Buccal Swabs," IEEE Conference on Technologies for Homeland Security, 2011.

279. Patrick Tucker, "Special Operators are Using Rapid DNA Readers," *Defense One*, May 21, 2015, available from *www.defenseone.com/technology/2015/05/special-operators-are-using-rapid-dna-readers/113383/?oref=defenseone_today_nl*.

280. Gefrides and Welch, "Forensic Biology: Serology and DNA," p. 39.

281. Isaacson *et al.*, "Robust Detection of Individual Forensic Profiles in DNA Mixtures," *Forensic Science International: Genetics*, Vol. 14, January 2015, pp. 31–37.

282. Eric Schwoebel, "Genomic Analysis and Human Identification," briefing slides and discussions with author, Lexington, MA: MIT Lincoln Laboratory, January 9, 2013. Also, Melissa

Gymrek *et al.*, "Indentifying Personal Genomes by Surname Inference," *Science*, January 18, 2013, available from *www.sciencemag.org/content/339/6117/321.full*.

283. Douglas Shontz, *DNA as Part of Identity Management for the Department of Defense*, Santa Monica, CA: RAND, 2010, p. 9.

284. David Pendall, *Global Operations and Biometrics: Next Generation Capabilities and Policy Implications*, Carlisle, PA: U.S. Army War College, 2013, p. 4.

285. Andrew Pollack, "Building a Face, and a Case, on DNA," *The New York Times*, February 23, 2015, available from *www.nytimes.com/2015/02/24/science/building-face-and-a-case-on-dna.html?_r=0*.

286. Pendall, p. 26.

287. Sandra I. Erwin, "As Defense, Intelligence Agencies Drown in Data, Technology Comes to the Rescue," *National Defense Magazine*, November 2014, available from *www.nationaldefensemagazine.org/archive/2014/November/Pages/AsDefenseIntelligenceAgenciesDrowninData,TechnologyComestotheRescue.aspx*.

288. Aparna Garg and Allan Ramsay, "Semantic Content Analysis of Video: Issues and Trends," W. Lin *et al.*, eds., *Multimedia Analysis, Processing & Communications*, Berlin, Germany: Springer-Verlag, 2011, pp. 443–457.

289. John, Markoff, "Researchers Announce Advance in Image-Recognition Software," *The New York Times*, November, 17, 2014, available from *www.nytimes.com/2014/11/18/science/researchers-announce-breakthrough-in-content-recognition-software.html?_r=0*.

290. Tom Simonite, "A Startup's Neural Network Can Understand Video," *MIT Technology Review*, February 3, 2015, available from *www.technologyreview.com/news/534631/a-startups-neural-network-can-understand-video/*.

291. For a discussion of this research, see Andrew Gallagher, Clint Mathialagan and Dhruv Batra, "VIP: Finding Important

People in Images," February 9, 2015, available from *www.arxiv.org/abs/1502.05678*.

292. Tom Simonite, "Google's Brain-Inspired Software Describes What It Sees in Complex Images," *MIT Technology Review*, November 18, 2014, available from *www.technologyreview.com/news/532666/googles-brain-inspired-software-describes-what-it-sees-in-complex-images*.

293. George Seffers, "Tag Teaming Big Data," *Big Data ebook*, Fairfax, VA: AFCEA International, 2014, p. 13.

294. Conor Dougherty, "Google Translate App Gets an Upgrade," *The New York Times*, January 14, 2015, available from *www.bits.blogs.nytimes.com/2015/01/14/google-translate-app-gets-an-upgrade/?hp&action=click&pgtype=Homepage&module=second-column-region&_r=0*.

295. Hardy, "Facebook Offers Artificial Intelligence Tech to Open Source Group."

296. Davey Alba, "The Startup That Helps You Analyze Twitter Chatter in Real Time," *Wired Magazine*, February 12, 2015, available from *www.wired.com/2015/02/luminoso/*.

297. Ben Shneiderman, Carsten Gorg, Chaomei Chen, Jim Thomas, John Stasko, and Pak Chung Wong, "Graph Analytics — Lessons Learned and Challenges Ahead," *IEEE Computer Graphics and Applications*, Vol. 33, No. 5, September/October 2011, pp. 18-29, available from *www.cs.umd.edu/~ben/papers/Wong2011Graph.pdf*.

298. William Campbell, Charlie Dagli, and Clifford Weinstein, "Social Network Analysis with Content and Graphs," *Lincoln Laboratory Journal*, Vol. 20, No. 1, 2013, pp. 61-81, available from *www.ll.mit.edu/publications/journal/pdf/vol20_no1/20_1_5_Campbell.pdf*.

299. David Stillwella, Michal Kosinskia, and Thore Graepel, "Private Traits and Attributes are Predictable from Digital Records of Human Behavior," Proceedings of the National Academy of Sciences, *Early Edition*, March 11, 2013, available from *www.pnas.org/cgi/doi/10.1073/pnas.1218772110*.

300. For one such example, see Ana-Maria Popescu and Marco Pennacchiotti, "A Machine Learning Approach to Twitter User Classification," Proceedings of the Fifth International AAAI Conference on Weblogs and Social Media, Association for the Advancement of Artificial Intelligence, 2011, available from *www. aaai.org/ocs/index.php/ICWSM/ICWSM11/paper/viewFile/2886/3262.*

301. These traits represent the so-called "big five," or the five-factor model of personality considered to be the most comprehensive, reliable, and useful set of personality concepts. For discussion of use of social media for personality analysis, see Daniele Quercia, David Stillwell, Jon Crowcroft, and Michal Kosinski, "Our Twitter Profiles, Our Selves: Predicting Personality with Twitter," available from *www.cl.cam.ac.uk/~dq209/publications/ quercia11twitter.pdf.*

302. Renaud Lambiotte and Michal Kosinski, "Tracking the Digital Footprints of Personality," Proceedings of the IEEE, Vol. 102, No. 12, December 2014, pp. 1934-1939, available from *ieeexplore.ieee.org/xpl/login.jsp?tp=&arnumber=6939627&url=http %3A%2F%2Fieeexplore.ieee.org%2Fxpls%2Ficp.jsp%3Farnumber %3D6939627.*

303. *Ibid.*

304. Siobhan Peters and Craig Denholm, "Channel: Protecting Vulnerable People from Being Drawn into Terrorism: A Guide for Local Partnerships," London, UK: Office for Security and Counter-Terrorism, Home Office, October 2012, available from *www.gov.uk/government/uploads/system/uploads/attachment_data/ file/118194/channel-guidance.pdf.*

305. Mark Townsend, "How a Team of Social Media Experts Is Able to Keep Track of the UK Jihadis," *The Guardian*, January 17, 2015, available from *www.theguardian.com/world/2015/jan/17/ social-media-british-jihadists-islamic-state-facebook-twitter.*

306. Katrin Bennhold, "Fertile Ground for Militancy in Hometown of Jihadi John," *The New York Times*, February 28, 2015, available from *www.nytimes.com/2015/03/01/world/europe/fertile-ground-for-militancy-in-hometown-of-jihadi-john.html?_r=0.*

307. *Social Network Analysis with Content and Graphs*, p. 73.

308. Jihun Hamm, Adam Champion, Guoxing Chen, Mikhail Belkin, and Dong Xuan, "Crowd-ML: A Privacy-Preserving Learning Framework for a Crowd of Smart Devices," Columbus, OH: The Ohio State University, Department of Computer Science and Engineering, January 11, 2015, available from *www.arxiv.org/abs/1501.02484*.

309. *Social Network Analysis with Content and Graphs*, p. 68.

310. Eric Schmitt, "U.S. Intensifies Effort to Blunt ISIS' Message," *The New York Times*, February 16, 2015, available from *www.nytimes.com/2015/02/17/world/middleeast/us-intensifies-effort-to-blunt-isis-message.html?_r=0*.

311. Derek O'Callaghan, Derek Greene, Joe Carthy, Maura Conway, Nico Prucha, and Padraig Cunningham, "Online Social Media in the Syria Conflict: Encompassing the Extremes and the In-Betweens," research paper sponsored by the Cybercrime Centers of Excellence Network and Science Foundation Ireland (SFI), August 13, 2014, available from *www.arxiv.org./abs/1401.7535*.

312. See discussion of the computational science and information science campaign plans in the *Technical Implementation Plan: 2015-2019*, Adelphi, MD: U.S. Army Research Laboratory, January 2015, available from *www.arl.army.mil/www/pages/172/docs/ARL_Technical_Implementation_Plan.pdf*.

313. Elizabeth Dwoskin, "Sleuthing Search Engine: Even Better Than Google?" *The Wall Street Journal*, February 12, 2015, available from *www.wsj.com/articles/sleuthing-search-engine-even-better-than-google-1423703464*.

314. Rita Boland, "Novel Big Data Reveals Global Human Behavior," *Big Data ebook*, Fairfax, VA: AFCEA International, 2014, p. 13.

315. For background information, see the homepage for the Institute for the Study of Violent Groups, available from *www.isvg.org/organization.php*.

316. Amelia Thomson-Deveaux, "Tracking 125,000 Incidents of Global Terrorism," *FiveThirtyEight*, January 23, 2015, available from *fivethirtyeight.com/features/the-paris-attacks-are-just-a-few-of-125000-entries-in-the-global-terrorism-database*.

317. *U.S. Army Training and Doctrine Command (TRA- DOC) Pamphlet (TP) 525-3-1, The U.S. Army Operating Concept: Win in a Complex World,* Fort Eustis, VA: TRADOC, 2014, p. 33.

318. Barrack Obama, National Security Strategy of the United States, Washington, DC: The White House, February 2015.

319. Rosa Brooks, "There's No Such Thing as Peacetime," *Foreign Policy*, March 13, 2015.

320. Lieutenant General Michael Barbero, Testimony before the House of Representatives Committee on Homeland Security Subcommittee on Cybersecurity, Infrastructure Protection and Security Technologies, Washington, DC, July 12, 2012.

U.S. ARMY WAR COLLEGE

Major General William E. Rapp
Commandant

*****

STRATEGIC STUDIES INSTITUTE
and
U.S. ARMY WAR COLLEGE PRESS

Director
Professor Douglas C. Lovelace, Jr.

Director of Research
Dr. Steven K. Metz

Author
Colonel Glenn J. Voelz

Editor for Production
Dr. James G. Pierce

Publications Assistant
Ms. Rita A. Rummel

*****

Composition
Mrs. Jennifer E. Nevil